FRITZ BULTMAN

a retrospective

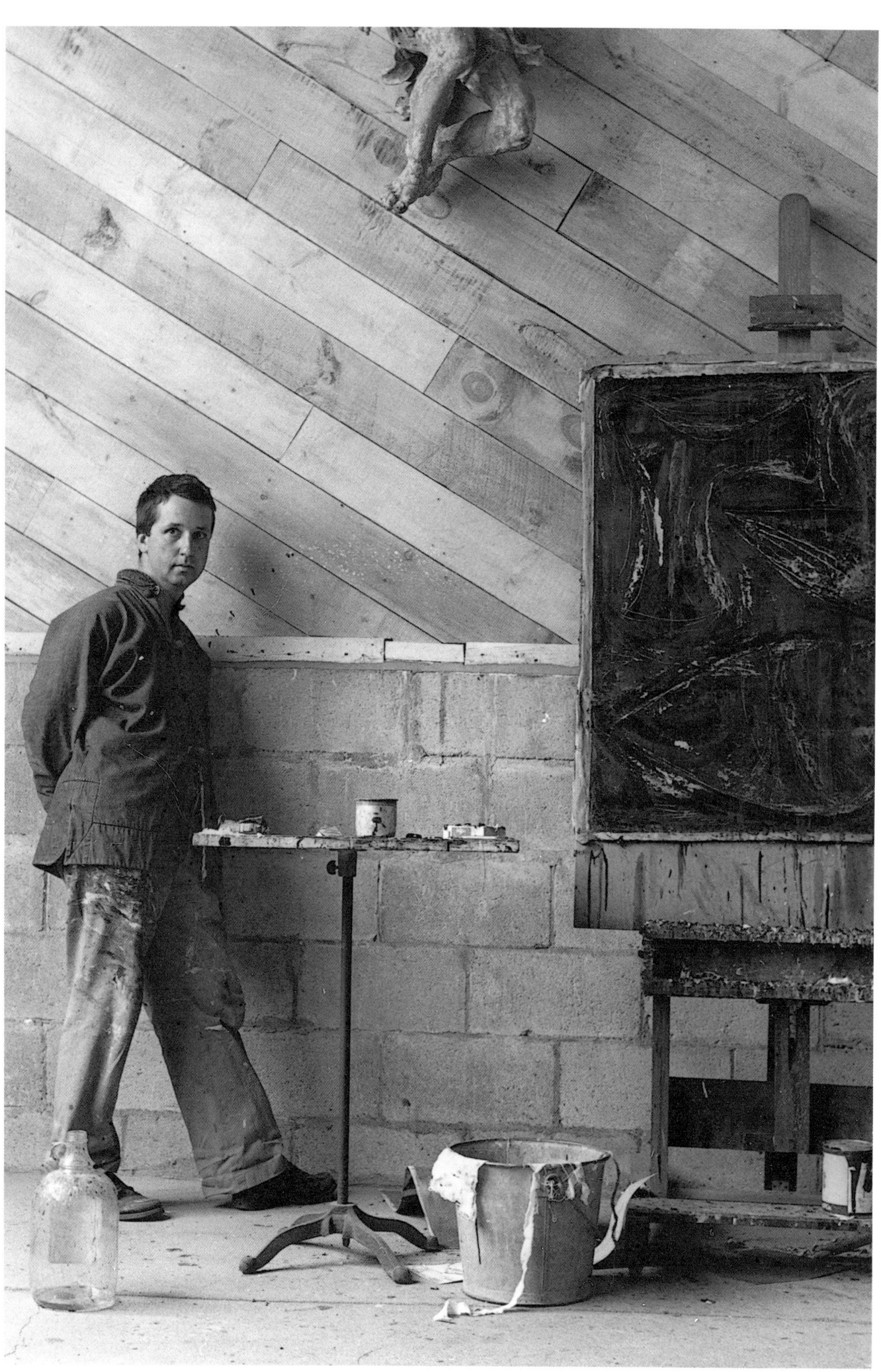

FRITZ BULTMAN

a retrospective

New Orleans Museum of Art

1993

EXHIBITION SCHEDULE

AUGUST 7 – OCTOBER 3, 1993
New Orleans Museum of Art

NOVEMBER 9, 1993 – JANUARY 2, 1994
Greenville County Museum
Greenville, South Carolina

APRIL 29 – JULY 10, 1994
Art Museum of Western Virginia
Roanoke, Virginia

SEPTEMBER 9 – OCTOBER 30, 1994
Provincetown Art Association and Museum
Provincetown, Massachusetts

3,000 copies of the catalog were published for the exhibition

FRITZ BULTMAN: a retrospective

Catalogue copyright 1993 New Orleans Museum of Art
Essay copyright 1993 April Kingsley/New Orleans Museum of Art
All rights reserved

Library of Congress Catalog Card Number 93-84177
ISBN: 0-89494-043-0

DESIGN: Eric Baker Design Associates, Inc., New York, New York

PHOTOGRAPHY: Personal Photos: Maurice Berezov, Renate Ponsold, Emerick Bronson
Photos of Work: Otto Nelson, Walter Russel, Ed Watkins, Charles Uht,
Malcom Varon, Geoffrey Clements

PRINTING: Red Ink Productions, Printed in Iceland

FRONT COVER: *The Hunter*, 1949, oil on celotex, 60 x 48

CONTENTS

In recent years the New Orleans Museum of Art has focused the public's attention on the outstanding achievements of talented artists from the city, state and region through a series of exhibitions, most of which were originated by the Museum. We are pleased to have presented either mid-career surveys or retrospectives of the work of Ida Kohlmeyer, Robert Gordy, Robert Warrens, Clementine Hunter, Sister Gertrude Morgan, Lynda Benglis and Evelyn Witherspoon. Other one-person exhibitions featured the artwork of Randell Henry, Emerson Bell, Frank Hayden, Walter Anderson, George Schmidt, Clarence John Laughlin, Caroline Wogan Durieux, Elizabeth Catlet, Trailer McQuilkin, Enrique Alferez, Keith Calhoun and Chandra McCormick.

This current in-depth examination of the paintings, collages, sculptures and drawings of Fritz Bultman continues that tradition. Even though he chose to live and work in New York City and Provincetown, he retained strong ties with his hometown, New Orleans.

Our Museum has had a long, continuing relationship with the Bultman family. Fritz's father A. Fred Bultman, Jr., served as a Trustee in 1943 and donated works of art to the Museum, the most notable a large 1939 painting, STILL LIFE, by Hans Hofmann. Fritz's sister, Muriel Bultman Francis, served on the Museum's Board of Trustees for nearly three decades and was ultimately elected its President and later an Honorary Life Trustee. Her magnificent art collection, which mainly concentrated on drawings by French 19th and 20th century masters, such as Ingres, Degas, Matisse and Braque, the work of Odilon Redon, the Surrealists and the New York School, was the subject of a 1985 NOMA exhibition, PROFILE OF A CONNOISSEUR, and was subsequently bequeathed to the Museum. Fritz Bultman and his wife Jeanne also have been most generous with gifts including African masks, German Expressionist woodcuts, and the complete portfolio of Henri Matisse's rare 1947 JAZZ. In 1974 NOMA mounted a special exhibition of forty of Bultman's marvelous figurative pencil drawings executed from the early 1960s to the early 1970s.

Fritz Bultman is recognized as a member of the First Generation of New York's Abstract Expressionists. Unfortunately, he was in Italy when the famous group portrait of these "Irascibles" was published in LIFE magazine and because of this quirk of fate, history has tended to overlook his inclusion in this artistic "fraternity." It is hoped this exhibition will help to reevaluate his artistic career and his role in the activity of this pivotal moment in American art history.

Exhibitions of this scope do not just happen. Many people have contributed to the project in various ways and we owe them a debt of gratitude for their assistance. Foremost, we wish to acknowledge the artist's widow Jeanne, whose wholehearted cooperation in making available her thorough records and files and photographs simplified our tasks immensely. Their sons Johann and Anthony have assisted in securing necessary loans. Art dealers Stephen L. Schlesinger in New York and Timothy Foley in New Orleans have provided valuable documentation on the artworks. A longtime friend and neighbor of the Bultmans, April Kingsley, spent many summers in Provincetown talking about art with him. She has produced a most insightful essay for this catalog and condensed the lengthy Irving Sandler interview with Bultman into a fascinating look into the life and times and thoughts of the artist. We thank Mr. Sandler for his generous permission to use his important interview. Robert Motherwell's tribute to his friend Fritz was prepared for this publication before his death in 1991 and we are pleased to present it here. Credit for the selection of the artist's writings published elsewhere in this catalog goes to Robert Lawlor.

We are grateful to Thomas W. Styron at the Greenville County Museum in South Carolina, Ruth Appelhof at the Art Museum of Western Virginia in Roanoke, and Robyn S. Watson at The Provincetown Art Association and Museum for their willingness to present the exhibition at their institutions. Our Museum's Registrar, Paul Tarver and his staff, and our Curator of Exhibitions, Dan Piersol and his staff, are to be commended for their careful attention to the logistics and handling of artworks necessary to the formation of the exhibition. We acknowledge Cecily Dixon for her superb editing of the catalog manuscript, B.H. Friedman for his useful advice, and Guy Walker and Anne Bittel for being there to handle all the myriad details of organization and assistance. Lastly but certainly not least, we are deeply grateful to all the lenders to the exhibition, listed elsewhere in this catalog, who have generously relinquished their possessions for this occasion. Needless to say, without their cooperation, the exhibition would not be possible.

We are privileged to have known Fritz and have long admired his work. It gives us great pleasure to be able to present a survey of his accomplishments as one of the first exhibitions in the new, expanded facilities of the New Orleans Museum of Art.

E. John Bullard,
director

William A. Fagaly,
assistant director for art

lenders

8

L E N D E R S

to the exhibition

Anka and Louis Begley, New York, New York

Anthony F. Bultman, IV, New Orleans, Louisiana

Bethany and Johann Bultman, New Orleans, Louisiana

Ciba-Geigy Corporation, Ardsley, New York

Clarence Cukor, Wilton, Connecticut

Mr. and Mrs. James S. Deely, New York, New York

William Frankel, Wynnewood, Pennsylvania

Abby and B. H. Friedman, New York, New York

Solomon R. Guggenheim Museum, New York, New York

Jo Ann Hirshhorn, Metairie, Louisiana

Hunter College of the City University of New York

Archer M. Huntington Art Gallery, University of Texas at Austin

Mrs. George P. Kramer, New York, New York

Ruth S. Latta, Provincetown, Massachusetts

The Montclair Art Museum, Montclair, New Jersey

National Museum of American Art, Smithsonian Institution, Washington , D.C.

Joan and Michael Nelson

The Roger Houston Ogden Collection, New Orleans, Louisiana

Robert W. Ossorio, New York, New York

Estate of Judith Rothschild, New York, New York

Vera and Stephen L. Schlesinger, New York, New York

Ronnie and John Shore, Cincinnati, Ohio

Pat Sloane, Brooklyn, New York

Vincent Smith-Durham, Embreville, Pennsylvania

Tulane University, New Orleans, Louisiana

Weatherspoon Art Gallery, University of North Carolina at Greensboro

Whitney Museum of American Art, New York, New York

The William Benton Museum of Art, University of Connecticut, Storrs, Connecticut

A TRIBUTE TO FRITZ

After forty years of acquaintanceship with Fritz Bultman and his work, I am still convinced that he is one of the most splendid, radiant and inspired painters of my generation, and of them all, the one drastically and shockingly underrated. I do not know why this is so. Perhaps, with his explosive temperament, he was not very adept at playing the New York gallery game. But whatever the reason for the neglect of his work, I still find it as radiant as ever, after all these years. I even have a color reproduction of one of his works hanging in the tiny Pantheon of other works that I admire, in reproduction, pinned to the wall of my studio. His work seems even more remarkable given the schlock and kitsch so prevalent in the contemporary art scene. His work represents a standard of sensibility, a background of the best of Modernism and a painting instinct that, if anything, is too good for the present day public.

ROBERT MOTHERWELL
19 october 1988

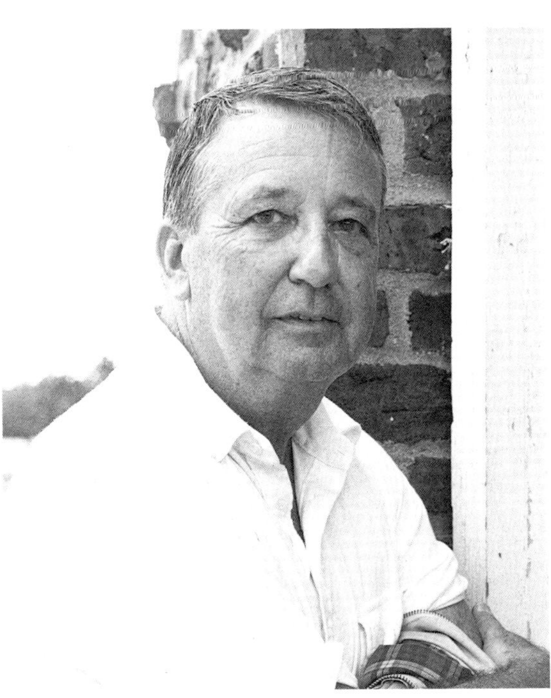

F R I T Z   B U L T M A N

by April Kingsley

Fritz Bultman's home in the Garden District of New Orleans was the setting for Tennessee Williams's play Suddenly Last Summer. Fritz's father created the two story glassed-over extension on the house which Williams, who was a guest of the Bultmans when he wrote the play, described this way;

> The interior is blended with a fantastic garden which is more like a tropical jungle, or forest, in the prehistoric age of giant fern-forests when living creatures had flippers turning to limbs and scales to skin. The colors of this jungle garden are violent, especially since it is steaming with heat after rain. There are massive tree flowers that suggest organs of the body, torn out, still glistening with undried blood; there are harsh cries and sibilant hissings and thrashing sounds in the garden as if it were inhabited by beasts, serpents and birds, all of savage nature....[1]

Lush beauty and sensuality in combination with primordial violence, nodes of extreme exoticism within the prosaic fabric of the quotidian, magic amid the mundane — this was the world Fritz Bultman came into and, no matter how physically distanced he was from it later in life, never left.

A(nthony) Fred Bultman III was born on April 4, 1919 into an old and well-respected family that ran the refined New Orleans funeral establishment known as The House of Bultman. His father was a proudly self-made businessman and an active force in the community who became involved in various architectural projects,[2] including the two-story tropical hothouse. He also collected antiques quite seriously, and had a wide range of male friends from esthetes to carpenters. His mother was a true southern belle, beautiful, imperious, and possessed of perfected social graces. She rose late, lingered over her toilette, and spent her days socializing and overseeing the functions of her home and staff. Young Fritz, usually in the care of his beloved nanny and the chauffeur, often played in the house of his favorite aunts, who owned pets which were forbidden at home. Dress up and play-acting occupied him when he wasn't going for rides with the chauffeur or visiting the wonder-full New Orleans zoo. It was a somewhat lonely childhood since his sister was older than he and well along in grammar school when he was born. In time-honored Freudian tradition father doted on Muriel while mother pampered her little boy. Fritz loved seeing his mother dressed up in elegant ball gowns and jewelry and would powder (or, on special occasions even paint) her already white skin even whiter for social events. The feeling for the swelled curve of a woman's back never left his hands for you can see it in the drawings he did of women until his death in 1985.[3]

Fritz Bultman's parents had strong cultural connections in New Orleans and far outside it. His mother aspired to a salon in the continental manner and Fritz remembered there being many homegrown as well as imported literary, musical, and artistic figures around his house all the time. During the summer of 1932 Morris Graves, a twenty-one year old burgeoning artist from the far away Puget Sound, lived with them, and his enchanting presence had the quality of a miracle for thirteen year old Fritz.[4] An inveterate story-teller, Graves regaled Fritz and his friends with marvelous tales of what he'd seen on his travels in the Pacific tropics and the Far East, always emphasizing the colorful flora and fauna. Capricious and unconcerned with boring bourgeois rules of propriety, Graves gave the young Bultman a new outlook on life. "There was a whole magic about everything he did," Fritz recalled.[5]

Graves often took Fritz with him to draw the birds in Audubon Park or the zoo, initiating the young teen-ager into a feeling for form he never lost. The pregnant curves and their counter pressures that characterize so much of Bultman's life's work can be readily seen in the earliest extant Graves works of around this time. Graves's M o o r S w a n, 1933, in the Seattle Art Museum, for instance, in which a few major curves put pressure on the compact, squarish, framing edge is prophetic of a strategy basic to Bultman's mature pictorial style. One of Bultman's last paintings, B l u e   W a v e, 1983, consists of a single large curving form within a squarish rectangle. Many later influences served to reinforce this highly sensual and empathetic sense of the life in forms and the forms in life, but I believe it began with Graves.

Other effects of this formative relationship can be traced as well. The paintings Graves was doing then were thickly encrusted with pigment applied with a palette knife. This must have made the active facture of the paintings of Fritz's later teacher, Hans Hofmann, seem perfectly natural since most of Fritz's paintings from the time he left art school until the late sixties are characterized by a rough, aggressive handling of the surface. Among his and Graves's jointly planned projects was a painting wholly in alizarin crimson to achieve deeply saturated color. Fritz did come close to such monochrome red intensity in a number of later paintings. Aside from paintings of birds, usually with long, sensually curving necks and wings, Fritz remembered Graves painting only one other subject, a room of prostitutes.

Bultman and Graves pored over the few reproductions they could find of paintings by Gauguin and Poussin, both of whom held a lifelong fascination for Fritz. In fact, late in life he purchased a John Graham painting entitled P o u s s i n M ' I n s t r u i t ("Poussin instructs me"),[6] the study of which may well give us a hint as to what Graves showed young Fritz about Poussin's art. Certainly it is important to note the way Graham emphasized the anatomical swellings and concavities with outlining and shading. Doing so makes them float like individual shapes at the same time that they remain body parts. This is one-of-a-piece with Graves's shaping of birds' wings and swans' necks and with the mature Bultman's way of carving beautiful, curved chunks of flesh out of the model with his drawing pencil. His knife-like line seems to cut matter out of space as though it were truly solid. Poussin's legacy was passed on to Ingres, whose sure handling of contour directly affected both Graham and Bultman.

It seems that after a few months the charming idleness and demi-decadence of the south wore thin for Graves who was accustomed to the rigors of the wild northwest. He later acknowledged being "happy and fortunate to be in such a home," but New Orleans, he said, "did not work out for me. The city brought me up against my upbringing. The Bohemian life, the sensuality, the endless talk, the lounging and postponements turned me away with a sense of contamination." Bultman, however, thrived in that languid air and brought it with him to New York. He never lost his slow, elongated, southern way of talking and his friends from home always remarked on how much his New York townhouse reminded them of his New Orleans home. In Manhattan[7] curved horsehair sofas, horned furniture (chairs, tables, footstools, mirror frames and hat racks), marble and wrought iron tables, Oriental rugs, decorative gilt mirrors, porcelain plant holders and vases, and elaborate Victorian cabinets were set amid a profusion of art from all periods and on all levels, from the so-called Primitive and the genuinely naive to the most exquisitely sophisticated and modern. His art fed—and thrived—on this dialogue with his furnishings and collections. The English painter Hogarth spent years on, and devoted a whole book to, the analysis of beautiful curved lines in the 18th century; Fritz lived among them. Around his studio he pasted postcards and reproductions cut from newspapers and magazines: bounteous nudes, birds on the wing, wrestlers, medieval Italian paintings, cowboy hats with their dramatically curved rims, elephant tusks, cacti, sculpted Greek nude athletes, cave drawings, horses in action, the pocked surface of a fungus, bellies, breasts, thighs, and Uccello's Battle of San Romano. When you look at the world through Fritz's eyes, beautiful lines are everywhere.

Prior to Graves's appearance, the precocious Bultman was led by his boyhood art teacher to an early appreciation of modern art. Various later teachers affected him as well, but Hans Hofmann was the premier influence throughout his life's work: in the execution, the richness of color, the fusion of geometry and painterliness, and even in the small matter of using dotted lines and other diagrammatic elements. Despite this, Bultman's paintings don't really remind one of Hofmann's. It's a curious paradox, explainable primarily by Bultman's seemingly innate "will to form" in certain, almost obsessive ways, and by the fact that other influences, such as that of Morris Graves, heightened these instincts. Another answer lies in Hofmann's own diversity. Hofmann painted in so many different ways in any given period that a one-person exhibition of his work could sometimes be mistaken for a group show. Bultman was a very consistent artist whose development took place in clear, slow stages; he varied his medium rather than his style. Then too, as exhibitions of paintings by Hofmann's students have demonstrated, their work doesn't tend to look like his.[8] George McNeil's painterly and coloristic virtuosity probably comes the closest to Hofmann's, but he is a figurative painter, and Hofmann, although he painted from life at least until the fifties, was not. Hofmann's teaching was multi-valent, it allowed the widest possible latitude, and thus produced artists as disparate as Wolf Kahn and Myron Stout.[9] The main thing his students learned, as Fritz put it, was how to have a "deep reverie about art."[10]

The differences between Hofmann's style and Bultman's are instructive. They both use paint in a thick, crusty manner (Bultman consistently and Hofmann inconsistently), but Bultman's surface facture is drier and far less ingratiating than Hofmann's. The oil in the paint seems to be the important thing for Hofmann; the pigment for Bultman. Also, Hofmann's colors are pure and sing out, whereas Bultman's are mixed, whitened, grayed, and glowering. Hofmann always seems to have painted with joy in his heart, but for Bultman the *pain* part of the word painting had more meaning. This is not true of his large, late collages however. There facture doesn't come into play, and Bultman's colors fairly burst with the Matissean spiritedness of Hofmann at his finest.

The diagrammatic look of Fritz Bultman's earliest paintings is closer to the drawings Hofmann made to illustrate the compositional principles of "push-pull" spatial interaction, than it is to Hofmann's paintings. A c t e o n   M a s k - S t i l l   L i f e, 1941, for instance, contains multiple overlapping and interacting picture-making systems using black and red lines, solid and dotted lines, triangular, circular and rectangular planes. Bultman titled a number of his early paintings to refer to the Actaeon myth — A c t e o n, D r e a m   o f   D e e r,   D o g   o f   A c t e o n, and T h e   H u n t e r. Actaeon was a hunter who was turned into a deer by Diana because he chanced to see her naked at her bath in the woods. He didn't wear a mask and there is no face-like aspect to A c t e o n   M a s k - S t i l l   L i f e. A reading as still life is more feasible, but a still life of what is impossible to ascertain. So, although he drew from life, as Hofmann instructed, he did not paint from life (or an idea of life, such as a myth), in Hofmann's direct, one-to-one manner. He was much more abstract or distanced from his subject, though not, perhaps, from its meaning.

Diana's beauty and Actaeon's punishment is a metaphor for the dangers facing the artist in the quest for beauty. If Actaeon represents a rejection of bonds with other men because of a desire for a female, what does it signify to be punished so cruelly for heterosexual love? Perhaps, Actaeon's discovery of Diana conflates the artist's discovery of art with the lover's erotic moment. The child's loss of innocent vision is the moment of discovery that transforms a child into an adult, a thrilling encounter relived again and again by the adult in every esthetic/erotic moment.

The Actaeon myth and Tennessee Williams's play S u d d e n l y   L a s t   S u m m e r have many psychological, romantic, sociological, and esthetic ramifications in common. Both end with the eating of a man's flesh[11] by the man's former victims or servants: the hunter becomes the hunted, the hero becomes the conquered, the perpetrator the victim, the powerful one the weakling. And when does this sexual role reversal occur? When we are out of control. When something or someone comes into our lives and overwhelms us, throwing us off course, out of kilter, into a frenzy, in a spin—we often call such occurrences romance. Cannibalism and other inhuman things humans do to each other are extreme cultural facts of life that are rarities now though they weren't in earlier ages. Our primitive social patterns and great social upheavals, such as the shift from matriarchal society to a patriarchical one, are recorded and metaphorically encoded in myths.[12] Fearsome female goddesses like Hera, Diana, Medusa, and the Furies reflect the anxieties of men during their transition to power when patriarchy took over. The fascination artists have with such subjects, of course, has definite psychological implications, but esthetically it has meaning as well. Willem de Kooning once said that "flesh was the reason oil paint was invented,"[13] a painter's credo that reveals the frisson of dread and desire (or fear and pleasure) felt at the thought of flesh being torn from a living body being transferred to the hand of a painter as it wields the brush. Thus, although Bultman didn't paint images of Actaeon, the manifold meaning of the myth fueled his esthetic ardor.[14]

The Hunter, 1949, is the final, grand statement of this theme. In it a form on the right similar to the one in Dog of Acteon, 1947, can be interpreted as attacking the larger, (antlered? fleeing?) personnage[15] on the left. Bloody orange-reds are the only interruptions in this bristling and violent, black and white canvas. Though he didn't title later paintings after this myth, it remained on his mind, and versions of some of the forms he found in which to express it appear in later works. An aggression of right side against left, attacking or pushing into it in the middle by crossing over from right to left along the midline, is a frequent pictorial action in subsequent paintings such as Interior Rain, 1953, the huge Gravity of Nightfall triptych, and Greek and July, both of 1962.

Cruciform configurations appear in each medium Bultman mastered—painting, sculpture, collage and drawing—at all points in his artlife. While vertical paintings of the late forties like The Black King and The Red King were divided into three registers, his more squarish surfaces[16] were usually composed in quadrants with a strong horizontal emphasis across the midline. The subjects of Maize Bird and the Reader paintings were different—the former a reference to corn grown in his Provincetown garden and the latter to a friend who lived in a shack on that property and posed for him while reading—but their compositions have this quadrant composition in common.

Like so many of the other Abstract Expressionist painting in the late forties, Bultman worked a great deal in black and white. This essentialization reflected the all-or-nothing threat of a nuclear holocaust, along with the fact that color was as yet uncommon in television, movies, advertising, reproductions and much of the rest of our artificial visual world. Today we take color for granted, but in 1950, things looked very black and white. The dealer Sam Kootz mounted a show that year titled "Black or White," including Bultman as well as Robert Motherwell, Bradley Walker Tomlin, Adolph Gottlieb, and Hofmann. In the exhibition catalogue, Motherwell spoke of white pigment being made of poisonous lead and black pigment coming from animals' bones or horns carbonized by fire; Fritz undoubtedly appreciated the idea.

Bultman, showing at the Hugo Gallery at that time, had just closed his February exhibition. Critic Belle Krasne mentioned his "darkly brooding, totemic abstraction" and "gouged-out surfaces" before going on to say:

There is something elemental in all of Bultman's canvases. The most recent,
MAIZE: THE HUNTER, is straight passion. Free, marked by a blood-
on-the-moon fierceness, the canvas strikes at the heart with plunging spears of juicy
red on splaying black and white.

If the show makes clear Bultman's energy it leaves open the question of
whether the artist can sustain a fever pitch without exhausting us along with him.[17]

Each critic reviewing Bultman's show had a completely different take on it. Stuart Preston, writing in the *New York Times*, praised Fritz's "remarkable power of organization," and noted the following about his compositions: "Lines and blank areas cross and combine with complexity, but the result is a welcome clarity that can be 'read' like a coat of arms with many quarterings."[18] Bultman's good friend Donald Windham wrote the catalogue note. Knowing his subject well he stressed Fritz's use of mythology (citing Actaeon) and symbols (citing the cross) to create "images which bear the weight of reflection on contemporary life." He called Bultman's paintings "yantras for the contemporary occident" which "would not be out of place in the church."[19] Weldon Kees, also a friend of Fritz's, but a critic writing disinterestedly in *The Nation*, didn't agree with Windham and said that religious content was "not apparent [in]" and "irrelevant to Bultman's work."[20] Interestingly, and prophetically, Kees noted that Bultman was "concerned with massive sculptural forms."[21] Not long after the exhibition Bultman left for Italy and an introduction to the art of bronze casting at the invitation of the Italian government.[22] Sculpture became an increasingly fertile area in which to work, and in the sixties and seventies he received a number of grants that enabled him to cast large-size bronzes.

Bultman's sculpture is probably the most classical and mythological part of his *oeuvre* as well as the most overtly religious. In front of his bronzes one often thinks of *The Nike of Samothrace* or of some other Greek goddess, god or athlete;[23] of the Crucifixion, an orant worshipping, or a saint. The works from the fifties look like objects that would serve some function in a pagan religious ritual. Their titles, Lunar, Solar, Triune, Vase of the Winds, indicate such a reading. Works from the sixties like Plant-Metamorphosis, 1963, have an aggressive, bristling quality and yet they often derive from and seem still a part of the plant world. The turning point in this medium seems to have come in the middle of the decade with the versions of Good News executed between 1963 and 1966. The significance of the Resurrection for a man who had just survived four major operations in two years (1963-64) is obvious. His anguish and his joy is fully expressed in the shift from the truncated forms of Good News I to the surging, twisting, upthrust and cantata-like rhythmical swellings of Good News II. The sculptures of the seventies such as Opening and Closing, 1974, and the Catch series soar well over nine feet in height and are smooth like leaves and bones. Creating out of reveries triggered by nature,[24] he worked directly in plaster, alternately building and carving on a wire mesh armature to produce these bronzes, which he described as having "the geometry of interior sensations."[25]

Sculpture and drawing being generally black and white mediums, color asserted itself in Bultman's paintings and collages. Reds predominate in his oeuvre after the forties, even in landscape-inspired paintings such as R o s a   P a r k, named for a pretty street in New Orleans, and the many versions of T r e m b l i n g   P r a i r i e, which came out of his never-forgotten experiences of the burning of the swamps in the delta. "What appears to be a sheet of water will be burning with very high flames against a blue sky," he told Irving Sandler, adding that he found the sight "terribly exciting." For Bultman the color red was fire, torn flesh, blood, and possibly tropical flowers. Red may also have signified the heat of passion, in anger, in love, or in the act of creation.

S k i n   o f   t h e   N e g r e s s, 1957, indicates another complex source of inspiration for Bultman. The direct impetus for the painting was a black dancer/model from Harlem named Claretta, whom Fritz loved to draw in the fifties. But his feeling for brown skin goes back to his boyhood love for his nursemaid.[26] His childish pleasure in occupying her ample lap is further conveyed in a series of sixties paintings titled T h e   L a p which are related to the 1957 painting compositionally, though painted much more tightly. T h e   C h a u f f e u r and T h e   N u r s e, two eight foot tall curved panels of 1968, are named in honor of the two black people so important to him as a child. Ocher figures strongly in both, as one might expect if he identified that color with brown skin. It also might be recalled that he loved Gauguin's paintings. The nocturnal light in so much of Bultman's painting, his way of tuning his color to brown rather than relating it to white, may have stemmed in part from Gauguin's similar practice in his paintings of brown-skinned Tahitian women.

After 1961 when blue figured prominently in M   O v e r   W, a work Fritz always counted among his most important, blue increasingly made its way into his paintings. It occurred as his edges became tauter, perhaps because blue is so atmospheric in painterly contexts and works better in hard-edged abstractions. Usually, however, blue was an intrusion into a field of red, brown (or ocher), and black. Blue started to dominate when his inspiration began to derive from water, as in the W a v e paintings, the last one of which, B l u e   W a v e, 1983, was entirely in blues.[27]

Red and yellow were the dominant colors in his collages from the outset with O l d   G o l d, 1938, made of found and painted papers. Formal characteristics, such as the tendency to symmetry, centrality, geometry with echoing curves, are present in his paintings as well. The primary difference between his work in the two media besides surface texture is the quality of the color, which is purer and more intense in his collages, then and always. Though he used some torn edges, most of Bultman's collages (before and after he was affected by Matisse's paper cutouts), were made with scissors. He used fairly heavy paper, often torn from spiral-bound pads with the perforations retained and used compositionally. The paper was coated with gouache varied in density by his brushwork. Since cut paper is of its nature hard-edged, blue readily found a place in his collages, even in the sixties when they were most rough, jagged, and thickly overpasted.[28] Blue predominates in the grand free-form collages of the seventies. Here, liberated at last from the limits of the framing edge, which had crowded him from the start in all three two-dimensional media (painting, collage and drawing[29]), Bultman fully came into his own: he was a master of the medium on the level of Matisse and Motherwell.

In fact Bultman's collages were even more compositionally daring and coloristically exciting than Motherwell's. Whereas Motherwell tended somewhat formulaically to stack or cluster a single group of elements in one perfectly placed spot on a field of solid color, Bultman's great collages of the seventies grew naturally outward from a starting point near the center and ended when they had to, stopping short of, or crossing out of, the rectangle if necessary. Ovals, "T" shapes, "Y"s—they all have a quality of inevitability because nothing is either filled in to cover the field, or not added on if it was needed. M a r d i   G r a s, an exuberant eight by four foot collage of 1978, is a marvelous example of this compositional freedom. The curving, figure-like brown form on the right is similar to the one in the righthand side of K i n g   Z u l u, a 1960 painting titled in reference to the figures in the annual Black Mardi Gras parade. Colored ocher and brown, probably because of its subject matter, this collage, and one or two in which green dominates, are unusual. Red, yellow and blue are the norm. The small colored squares in his collages establish alternate linear systems within each work. Like the spiral pad perforations, they are carryovers from the dotted lines of his early paintings. From the celebratory look of these works, collage seems to be the medium in which Fritz was happiest working.

Drawing and painting fuse in the collages. For example, the 1962 drawing U n o, the 1961 painting M   O v e r   W (turned on its side), and the 1962 painting J u l y, all seem to hover inside his 1962 collage L o v e r s. Perhaps Fritz considered M   O v e r   W so important because in it he was able to make the impossible work for him and get the M superimposed on the W. Doing so he created an interlocked unit like the infinity symbol, or the yin/yang knot, or—and this would hardly have been lost on him—two people in the act of intercourse. Its function in the L o v e r s collage suggests so. Occasionally drawing and sculpture meld, for example in V i c k i - B r i d g e   I, 1972; or collage and sculpture images coincide. This occurred in the B a r r i e r sculptures which are pre-figured in the B a r r i e r (or I l i u m / T h e   B u r n i n g   o f   T r o y) collages of 1966, made after a trip to Greece. The fusion of painting and sculpture is a more complex issue in Bultman's oeuvre. In 1947 he painted a pair of canvases titled S c u l p t u r e   S t u d y   I   &   I I which resemble seated figures in profile; and other painted images of the Forties, like the M a i z e   B i r d, certainly have a sculptural feel. Aspects of the Actaeon/hunter configurations reappear in the 1958 bronze A z o r e s. T h e   C r a d l e, a 1958 sculpture,[30] recalls the curves of I n t e r i o r - R a i n, 1953, and looks ahead to numerous circling, thrusting images, all the way from J u l y, 1962, to the very late B l u e   W a v e of 1983.

Two other aspects of the interaction between painting and sculpture need to be addressed here. The first is Bultman's use of curved panels in 1968 for the paintings, T h e   C h a u f f e u r and T h e   N u r s e. Eight feet high and curving out over one's head, these panels are also tapered down considerably from their four foot top width. Thus they are out of square and sculptural in two ways while still not being reliefs. In his interview with Irving Sandler, Bultman mentions his admiration for David Alfaro Siquieros's enormous, multi-medium M a r c h   o f   H u m a n i t y in Mexico City adding, "I have always felt that maybe the juxtaposition of sculptures and paintings, of making walls of paintings and sculptures, somehow they could eventually lead to an interior architecture, or an articulation of an outdoor space."[31] He attempted such a *gesamtkunstwerk* in 1965 when he painted G o o d   N e w s   I I - D e p a r t, a wall-size, four panel painting intended as a foil for G o o d   N e w s   I I, 1964-66, a three part sculpture complex that is seven feet high and eight feet wide overall. The reference to the good news for humankind imparted by Christ's resurrection is a rare instance of specifically biblical subject matter in Bultman's work. The central element's outstretched "arms" speak both of the Crucifixion and of the release of the Resurrection. Likewise, the lateral units can be seen as the thieves on either side of Christ, or as jubilant announcers of the "good news." Curving to either side as they do, they echo the lateral outward movements in the painting, just as the sensuous curves of the central sculpture element are repeated in the waving central planes of the painting.

During the first quarter century of his career, Fritz would push himself to the point of exhaustion in painting until a new image would reveal itself to him. In that potent moment, which he described as "a sort of ecstasy of change," the painting became a kind "motion picture,"[32] one form seeming to grow out of another probably like a time-lapse film of a plant flowering. After his severe, life-threatening illness in the mid-sixties, and perhaps due in part to the heavy medication he took thereafter, Bultman's entire way of working changed so that he worked slowly in all four of his mediums simultaneously. From then on contour controlled everything as he moved freely from painting to sculpture to collage, exploring the various possibilities of a given shape. Drawing from a nude model became a direct source of these contours when he wanted to determine them in a deliberate fashion instead of letting them surface out of his unconscious, that "inner world of dreams and fantasy of the automatic, of metaphor, and of symbol." In his journal notes he described what happened through drawing this way:

> The vase [or vessel] quality of the female body was the first that forced itself into my conscious mind, then the wave meander, then the [twined] ropeness of the twisted torso and arms in space. Now I see a knot that sometimes the hips, thighs, and legs create..[33]

The wave meander is like the infinity symbol closed up and is directly related to the yin/yang symbol; twining is spiraling, and the spiral is nature's most elemental form because it results from the action of water, and water is essential to all lifeforms.[34] When a meander is squared off and crossed with itself it forms a swastika. The swastika is a cross[35] (or the cross is a swastika without its right-angled extensions). A cross inscribed in a circle is the world and a cross below a circle is the sign for female. No wonder Fritz described these particular symbols as "cabalistic, protean, and universal,"[36] and no wonder he used them so often in his work. "Painting to become universal," he said, "must release more and more of these magic signs to the spectator."[37]

We have seen some of the ways in which Bultman used the cross in his early paintings, but it shows up often in the drawings and paintings of the fifties and it is basic to much of his sculpture. A crossing of forms is present in almost every piece of his sculpture, but it is the main thrust of Lunar II, 1958, Vase of the Winds I, 1959, Hope and Portage, 1973, Garden at Nightfall I, 1975, and, of course Good News II.[38] Fritz was a profoundly religious man who his friend, the painter Ron Gorchov, described as "an enlightened Catholic, like T.S. Eliot."[39] He looked at religion in a universal, philosophical way rather than narrowly and pedantically, seeing connections between the many varieties of mythologies and rituals. The cross was a generic symbol with a host of meanings for him.

The wave meander and its offspring, the infinity and yin/yang symbols, are also present in various guises throughout Bultman's work from the fifties on. The pivotal point seems to have come in a painting titled The Sleeper of 1952 where the orbs or circular units he had been working with since the late forties are connected by swirling lines into a kind of figure eight[40]/infinity symbol. Ten years later he came back to using double curves, and all manner of waving, encircling lines. The works' titles— The Knot, The Lap, and Wave —indicate their source in the female models from whom he was drawing. This continues with varying degrees of explicitness as an infinity-yin/yang symbol (Three Waves Blue on Black, 1975, and Wave III, 1974), or suggestiveness as a sinuous female body. Bultman always maintained the importance of the erotic element[41] in drawing from the model and he manages to successfully carry that element over into late paintings like Big Blue Wave with Red and Big Blue Wave II of 1977.

The artist's role, as I believe Fritz Bultman saw it, was to mediate between the evanescent, epiphanous experience in all its complexity, and the reality of the physically created formworld. It was a role he could only play in the "deep reverie" Hans Hofmann encouraged, transfixed in a state bordering on ecstasy. The curl of a wave or of a tendril in his garden, the arch of a woman's back or the swelling of her hip, the unfurling of a chrysalis or the sharply terminated curves of a crown of thorns—a host of things in the world might send him into such a state. Childhood memories,[42] a life full of unusual experiences[43] and unusual people,[44] mythological concepts, religious rituals and images[45] —all the material of that "interior dialogue" from which he so thankfully "rested" when he worked directly from life—had the same effect of putting him in a chaotic and emotionally-charged state of mind. Only the process of working brought relief. "Art brings balances out of inequalities," he wrote, "visions and order out of chaos."[46]

> It is the work that sustains me; the continual opening outward. The forms and the results are secondary. It is the experience of the work that changes and directs life and gives it meaning.[47]

NOTES

1 Tennessee Williams, "Suddenly Last Summer," *The Theatre of Tennessee Williams,* (New York: A New Directions Book, 1990), p. 349. Actually there were no "massive tree flowers" in the garden, though it did feel decidedly jungle-like. Also, Williams wrote that the house was a Victorian mansion when it was really a Greek Revival structure dating from the mid-nineteenth century.

2 During the forties he moved the three buildings that had comprised his father's livery business and the funeral home together to make one huge establishment and faced the whole with a grand, white colonnade.

3 Tennessee Williams seems to have modeled various aspects of some of his characters after the Bultman family. Fritz's father (as well as his own) was reflected in Big Daddy in *Cat on a Hot Tin Roof.* Some of the quality of the relationship between Fritz's mother and sister can be discerned in *The Glass Menagerie* as well, and the fragile imperiousness of Fritz's mother is apparent in the role of Mrs. Venable in *Suddenly Last Summer.*

4 Fritz remembered the year as 1931 and his age as eleven or twelve instead of thirteen, but as Graves was 21 until August 28, 1932 we will hold to the 1932 dating of the New Orleans trip in the Whitney Museum of American Art's Morris Graves retrospective catalogue of 1956.

5 All quotes unless otherwise cited are from Irving Sandler's 1968 interview with the artist.

6 Fritz knew John Graham since 1937 probably through Lee Krasner. They had intense exchanges of ideas on and off over the years by letter and in person until Graham's death in 1962. A friend of Fritz's, Ron Gorchov, who was close to Graham in the late fifties, helped him get travel money by arranging sales of his paintings. Muriel Bultman bought two of Graham's works at this time which she bequeathed to the New Orleans Museum of Art in 1986. Fritz bought the 1944 painting *Poussin M'Instruit* in 1971.

7 Many of the same kinds of furnishings and art objects are also in the Provincetown house and guest house. Fritz's father was the source for a number of the antiques in the New York house.

8 Most of Hofmann's students simply didn't know much about his work so they didn't imitate it. It was deliberate on his part not to let the students into his studio, but also public exhibitions of his work were infrequent during the years he had a heavy teaching schedule.

9 Myron Stout was a close, lifelong friend of Fritz's and, though their work looks very different, they shared a love of curves that bordered on the obsessive.

10 Quoted in Cynthia Goodman, *Hans Hofmann and his legacy*, exhibition catalogue, Lever/Myerson Galleries Ltd., October 15-December 12, 1986, n.p.

11 It may be remembered that Williams described some of the flowers in the Bultman conservatory garden as looking like bloody organs torn from the body.

12 Frazer's *The Golden Bough* was the bible for scores of artists in the forties according to Robert Motherwell, but Ron Gorchov said that he and Fritz talked about myths and mythology by the hour during the fifties and well into the sixties. It was also a favorite topic of conversation with Myron Stout.

13 For Fritz it might be the pencil instead of oil paint.

14 This subjective subject matter, this painting out of your emotional unconscious, was what Robert Motherwell, Mark Rothko, William Baziotes and David Hare tried to teach in the Subjects of the Artists school in 1948-49. It was the esthetic basis of Abstract Expressionsim which is why the artworks produced by the movement's artists are so very different one from another stylistically.

15 The "figure" on the left has a dual form, half humanoid, half deer, the deer part being antlered and red.

16 It should be noted that Bultman often painted on board instead of canvas, as was Hofmann's practice.

17 Belle Krasne, "Fritz Bultman Bows," *Art Digest*, Feb. 15, 1950, p.15.

18 Stuart Preston, "Abstract Painting Heads Week's Art," *The New York Times*, Feb. 4, 1950, p.13.

19 This is prophetic in the light of Fritz's late work on the chapel in The House of Bultman.

20 He was right about appearance, but not about relevancy. Religious content becomes overt in some sculpture of the seventies and in many of the two-stage, collage/stained glass window pieces of the seventies and eighties. The only site-specific religious setting for such works, however, was in the chapel of the House of Bultman. The largest stained glass installation is in the Kalamazoo College in Michigan. It is an enormous and ecstatically celebratory multi-unit work which would certainly not be out of place in a church.

21 Weldon Kees, "Art," *The Nation*, February 4, 1950, p. 113.

22 Fritz was in Italy when the photograph was taken of "The Irascibles," the group of advanced artists who wrote to the Metropolitan Museum in May 1950 protesting the museum's anti-modern policies and programs. He had signed the letter, but the photograph, which was published in *Life* magazine January 15, 1951, has become such a famous touchstone of the movement that Fritz's absence from it has made it easy for him to be left out of discussions and exhibitions of Abstract Expressionism in subsequent years.

23 The last trip Fritz took was to Sicily to see the great Greek bronzes that had been unearthed there.

24 His Provincetown garden, particularly at nightfall, was a vital stimulus for these reveries, as were the beaches, dunes and woods of the area.

25 Fritz Bultman, "Footnotes to the Exhibition," in *Fritz Bultman, Bronze Sculpture 1963-1975*, January 10-February 7, 1976 Martha Jackson Gallery exhibition catalogue, n.p.

26 It may also have a source in his love of Gauguin's paintings. Gauguin was always at his coloristic best when he was working with brown skin instead of white.

27 The wave image was also derived from the female figure. This aspect is quite evident in *Wave II*, a sculpture idea which exists only in plaster maquette form. In it one curving torso-lap-leg unit supports a smaller, double-curving wave-body.

28 The Abstract Expressionist collage, as it was handled by so many in the so-called second generation of the movement, resembled Fritz's in these regards. The predominately yellow collages of John Grillo (another Hofmann student) are particularly close, though Bultman's results were never amorphous the way Grillo's were.

29 Interestingly, Bultman also began to draw more freely at this time, adding pieces of paper onto the original rectangle whenever he felt the need to carry a line off or out of the field. (Ingres, his drawing idol, had, in fact, done the same thing a century before.) Both collage and drawing now approximated his sculpture in this growing out, additive quality. Besides making the large plasters for his bronze sculptures on freeform armatures that he could alter at will by addition or subtraction, he was making sculptures out of sheets of black wax which he tore into pieces and used as though he was making a collage in space. Only in the medium of oil paint did he continue to struggle with the confining picture edge.

30 And to a lesser extent, *Lunar I*, 1951, one of his earliest sculptures.

31 Fritz wrote a lengthy piece (which was given as a speech in New Orleans in 1976) on the subject of fountains. He saw it as sculpture's mandate to address the "visual poverty" of urban and suburban America and to make a "bridge" to the daily life of its people. Fountains could accomplish this, fountains for people to congregate around, for children to play in, for people to wash their cars in, fountains that were sculptures in daily use. His model for one of these was an outdoor example of a totally encompassing work of art.

32 Fritz Bultman, "The Role of the Artist," in the exhibition catalogue, *Works by Fritz Bultman*, The Bertha and Karl Leubsdorf Art Gallery, Hunter College, September 15-October 23, 1987, p. 11.

33 Hunter College catalogue, p. 11.

34 "Water tends to form into spheres; even when moving it attempts to retain this spherical principle through circulation. Moving along spiralling surfaces, which glide past one another in manifold winding and curving forms, it expresses the conflict between its own natural inclination to the sphere and the force of gravity acting upon it." This is the central thesis of a book Fritz loved and recommended to all of his friends: Theodor Schwenk's *Sensitive Chaos* (New York: Schocken Books, 1965), p. 20.

35 It was an early Christian cross in the second and third centuries. It has also been sacred to Buddhists.

36 The full quotation on page nine of the Hunter College exhibition catalogue reads thusly: "The strongest symbols are those that have evolved over long periods of time: the +, the 00, the Greek alphabet, Chinese characters, the ʘ, the + . These are cabalistic..."

37 Hunter College catalogue, p.9.

38 *The Coat of Male*, 1963-1972, and *Barrier*, 1971, are cruciform but that doesn't seem to be central to their meaning.

39 From a conversation about Fritz with Ron Gorchov on January 5, 1973.

40 He was quite friendly with Franz Kline by this time and owned a 1951 painting of his. It is possible that Kline's painting *Figure Eight*, 1951, had an effect on him despite the lack of resemblance between their handling of the image.

41 The erotic element was extremely important to two very different artist-friends whose work Fritz collected: John Graham and Joseph Cornell. Cornell who lived in a world of suppressed desire and unbearable longing for the unattainable—namely non-familial love—expressed his feelings in works that were like love letters. Graham, who had a seemingly insatiable appetite for the female sex, pursued his ladyloves obsessively in his paintings.

42 One can speculate that growing up in a funeral home Fritz might have seen and heard any number of things which might have haunted his mind for the rest of his life.

43 Such as meeting Adolph Hitler because he was out hiking in the woods near Berchtesgaden with some friends and ran into the American Nazi Putsie Hofstaengle, Hitler's informal emissary to Americans abroad, who insisted that the young boys come into the house and shake hands with the German leader.

44 To cite only one of the hundreds of fascinating people Fritz and Jeanne Bultman counted among their friends, there was Charles James, the king of dress design among the cognoscenti.

45 Particularly St. Sebastian and other images of violent martyrdom.

46 Hunter College catalogue, p. 20.

47 From Bultman's notes.

FRITZ BULTMAN

On His Influences

On January 6th 1968 art historian Irving Sandler interviewed Fritz Bultman in the artist's New York townhouse/studio. The thirty-eight page typescript of that interview (which was apparently concluded mechanically when the tape ran out), is on file at the Archives of American Art, the Smithsonian Institution, Washington D.C. I have condensed it drastically, concentrating on three areas: Fritz's early life in New Orleans and the influence of Morris Graves and of Mexican art on him there; his German experience and the Chicago Bauhaus; Hans Hofmann's circle and New York in the forties, which was, as Fritz put it, "the world I had always wanted to know." In the interest of brevity I have summed up Irving's questions and elided Fritz's repetitions and backtracking when they were responsive rather than self-generated.

APRIL KINGSLEY

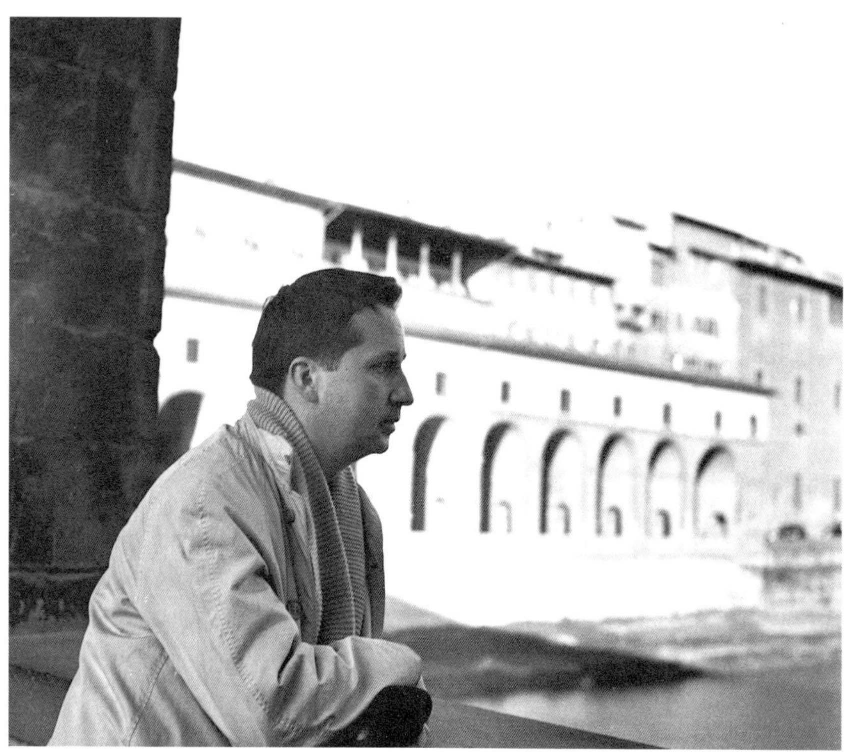

Irving tells Fritz that he always felt a sense of place emanating from his work and asks him about his early years growing up in New Orleans. Fritz responds: "It's always there. Friends from New Orleans come here to the house and they say, 'Well, you're still living at home.' I do." He talks about how much the family funeral business meant to him and his sister Muriel and how he keeps close contact with New Orleans where his children attend school. One childhood memory stands out in his mind:

> There's one very clear thing that occasionally you see there and you understand it completely. They try to burn the swamps down there and what appears to be a sheet of water will be burning with very high flames against a blue sky. And just the sight of this I find terribly exciting. I don't know anything else that seems to me as beautiful as that.

Fritz became interested in art at a very early age, eight to ten years old. "Two things happened," he says.

> First, I was in the Newman [grammar] school and there was an art teacher by the name of Marcelle Peret. She was a woman of considerable patience and understanding and interest in art, but more particularly in modern art. And very early, pre-high school, she started a Saturday morning painting class. And it seemed to me very natural and a means of working in a way that was compatible with any innocence that I had. Then, right after that, a friend of my family brought Morris Graves to New Orleans. Graves was at that time about twenty-one. I was about twelve. He had been sick. He had had the beginnings of tuberculosis and had been staying with an aunt in Texas for a number of years though his family lived then in Washington. First he stayed with these friends, then he stayed with my family. And he really sparked a tremendous interest in modern painting. I had by then seen a reproduction of a Gauguin in the Encyclopedia Britannica. I remember it very well. This painting, the color in it, and everything else had awakened my interest.

Irving notes that Fritz's family sound highly cultured, but Fritz says they weren't happy about his desire to be a painter "because they were business people and they thought— it was the Depression years—they thought painting was something you would do on the side. There were many writers around the house, and musicians, but there started a very early struggle about whether I was going to be painter, or an architect doing painting on the side."

Fritz never had the traditional academic background in art.

> In high school I started to go to a small school in New Orleans called the Arts and Crafts Club. The teachers there, though very thorough, were all modern-minded men. One of them was Paul Ninas; the other was Weeks Hall who had been a

student of Arthur Carles. And the third was a man by the name of Charles Bean, who though a rather academic painter himself was of a very much more open mind.

Irving notes that meeting Morris Graves when he was only twelve probably also made a big impact on him.

That's right. First, he was extremely stimulating and full of imagination. He loved to fabricate stories, some of which were pure fantasies and one never knew whether he was telling a story or the complete and utter truth. He was marvelous. There was a group of friends of mine from New Orleans and we all enjoyed and admired Morris because he had really at that age [21] made the step towards being a painter and was completely committed to it.

He had already been to the Far East several times as a seaman and he liked it in all of its colorful aspects. I would say at that point he was much more involved in its colorful aspects. Then later he's gotten into these more mystical things, but at that point Morris was involved in the color, in the exotic—I would say more in the decor of the tropics and the Far East—the flora, the fauna, everything interested him. We used to go to the Audubon Park and draw birds together. And there was a whole magic about everything he did. Finally, he and a friend of his and my father and I drove across the Southwest in a car with a rumble seat that we were taking out for my sister. It was the Depression time and it seemed in many ways a more spacious world than today. And even though no one had any money there was a great deal of, I would say, magic in the air for someone like Morris. He was able to move around. He would say on this trip back when we'd be going through the most desolate desert, "Give me five dollars and I'll beat you all back to LA." That's the sort of thing that he would do.

New Orleans was still very old-fashioned and proper then. I remember one Sunday afternoon being out riding in this same car with the rumble seat and we passed Morris walking down St. Charles Avenue, and when he hopped into the car he said we'd have to go to this and this place because he threw his shoes behind the bushes so he could walk barefoot. All of this was revealing of a completely different world than the totally bourgeois one that I seemed to know from my childhood.

Fritz denies any interest in the mystical side of Graves.

At that point he painted very, very heavily encrusted paintings with a palette knife. And they were of birds, always of birds, [though] I remember one very thinly painted picture of women—prostitutes in a room—that he had done. But the overriding interest that we had then [which] has been a lasting interest for me was Gauguin and Poussin. Morris seemed to be much more involved in painting as painting in those days. He talked about painting a whole canvas alizarin crimson, I remember, and this was like a desire on his part for a saturation of color. And these would be mutual projects, something that we wanted to do. In many ways this initial exposure to the

subject matter of painting and the object matter was very natural to me in the
surroundings where I had grown up—the heat, the color, the whole life down there
it was part of.

Irving asks Fritz whether he ever had any interest in social realist or regionalist art during the thirties, but Fritz says that "in New Orleans there was much more contact with Mexico than with the American regionalists." He mentions a Mexican sculptor:

> I think he must be a pure blood Indian, Enrique Alferez, who worked in New
> Orleans during this time, and he was a very, very good craftsman. Enrique was and
> still remains a friend of my family's. Through him and Paul Ninas the main work that I
> got to know was Posada. I have still the book of woodcuts that Rivera did the
> introduction to of Posada's that was issued about that time. And Rivera and Orozco
> were very, very important influences. I have tremendous admiration for the Mexican
> muralists. The scope of their work seemed correct to me. They really pre-saw the
> large scale painting in this country. I like the idea of this thing that Siquieros is doing
> now, this huge thing with sculptures sticking out of it in low bas relief, full bas relief. I
> have always felt that maybe somehow the juxtaposition of sculptures and paintings,
> of making walls of paintings and sculptures, somehow they could eventually lead to
> an interior architecture, or an articulation of an outdoor space.
>
> There was a certain conflict. It was really between that part of the South—
> the dampness and lushness of the city and of the swamps, the bayous, the trembling
> prairies—and the Southwest [of the Mexicans] that was called "dry" to me, the arid
> world. They're polarities that one was aware of—I was aware of at a very young age.
> My early work was involved with these polarities and they remain rather constant.

Irving brings back the contradiction inherent to Fritz's dual fascination with both Gauguin and Poussin. Fritz adds, "and Orozco. But it's out of this sort of contradiction that I try to resolve [these polarities]. I try to see what was the common denominator that this early interest started, because they all seem to have at least something in common and that something is stronger than what separates them. It's the fire and water. You very seldom see them together in such close juxtaposition as you do when they're burning a swamp."

PART II

Fritz went to Germany in 1935:

> This was called the Junior Year in Munich, and they were to get me into what I
> hoped would be the Bauhaus. When we got to Germany I discovered that the
> Bauhaus had been closed by Hitler, and I began to understand a few things that were
> going on in the modern world. I quickly got thrown out of that school. The people
> that ran it were totally unfriendly, let's say, to art. I had gotten a book on Cezanne. It
> was the first chance I had to see a lot of books on modern art. There were a couple
> of reproductions in it of drawings, and one of them was of two women, two nudes,
> probably from one of his Bacchanal things. The wife of the director of this group
> slammed the book shut, saying, "This is revolting." I realized these weren't my sort of
> people. Being kicked out was the best thing in the world that ever happened to me,
> although I was only sixteen at the time.

Irving and Fritz establish that Hans Hofmann was already in this country by then. Fritz
says that Hofmann's wife made one of the first transatlantic telephone calls in 1932 to tell
her husband not to come back to Germany.

> And Mrs. Hofmann had dissolved the school and a friend of mine, Peggy Huck (she
> later translated some of Hofmann's writings), was living in the Hofmann apartment.
> When she left I rented it from Miz [pronounced "meets," Mrs. Hofmann's nickname]
> and lived there a while. It was a marvelous apartment. African sculptures, plants, and
> there were all of her Vivins [a naive French painter]. Everything was there.
>
> All through 1936 and 1937 I lived with Miz Hofmann in her apartment and
> she took care of me, because I was still a kid. My father very wisely at the time when
> I got thrown out of school said either you sink or you swim. And so I was on my
> own. I soon learned how to swim, and she was a tremendous help. I learned a great
> deal from her. I learned about what a dollar meant and how to really make it go as
> far as you can make it go. I learned a lot from her.
>
> I started going to school on my own with tutors because I was trying to
> make the bridge, to know enough German and enough mathematics to get into one
> of the [technical schools there] or M.I.T. I had gotten to know Franz Roh who had
> been a friend of [Walter] Gropius and Moholy [Nagy]. [Both taught at the Dessau
> Bauhaus.] Munich was a very small place. Roh had already been in a concentration
> camp because of his modern leanings. I became aware of the totally forbidden life of
> modern art, the underground. That was really underground. You went around to see
> other painters' work—people like Fritz Winter who lived in the country, and
> another painter who could not exhibit. There would be great exhibits of Degenerate
> Art and Art de Kunst with marvelous Expressionist paintings in them. And one
> learned then that it can become very forbidden very suddenly. This whole
> background began to interest me very, very much.

Fritz tells Irving that Franz Roh wrote a whole series of letters to Fritz's father saying, "Please let him be a painter, don't fight this thing out," because it was a constant battle between father and son over whether Fritz would be an architect or a painter. "Finally," Fritz says, "the compromise came through the Bauhaus, the New Bauhaus that was opening in Chicago. And so I came back from Germany to go to school there. Which had been my reason for going to Germany." Irving asks for more information about the New Bauhaus.

> Well, it started off with Moholy Nagy and [Gyorgy] Kepes, and a man named Breidendick who ran the workshop. There were professors from the University of Chicago who gave courses in what was really the philosophy of the school, semantics, and every aspect of philosophy that fortified the Bauhaus position that everything could be taught, everything could be learned, everything could be understood, that nothing in the way of metaphysics existed or need exist in the world of art. This was disillusionment number one [for me]. Fortunately Archipenko taught there too. There was a lot of fanfare about it at that time.

Fritz explains that the school was really beginning to focus on architecture and that Moholy's inability to handle the finances brought it down. "He spent all the money immediately on renovating this old Marshall Field house on Prairie Avenue in rather interesting but unnecessary ways that we understand now. [Instead] the place where most everything took place was in the stables which was the sculpture studio. It was a marvelous facility there, just a stable." Then Fritz goes into more detail about the problems at the New Bauhaus:

> There was a real German rigidity and heavy-handed[ness]. Things got to a point of really rather childish discipline for fairly mature people. I was one of the youngest there. Tony Smith, Gerry Kamrowski, Dick Copy, Art Segal — there were a number of mature people. And they wanted to run it then on a rather rigid basis. The studios were closed on weekends because there was no supervision of students and they were afraid there would be romances in school and the school could not take responsibility for that. There was all that sort of nonsense. It just built up and finally there was a tremendous explosion at the end of the year. A lot of the students dropped out. One group went to study with [Frank Lloyd] Wright—Tony, Ted Van Fosson and Cuneo, who was a photographer, went to Wright. And then another group of us came to study with Hofmann—Gerry, [George] Mercer, and quite a number of people. The only thing you can say is that it just blew apart.

When asked why he chose to study with Hofmann, Fritz seems to imply that it was because Hofmann represented the opposite end of the spectrum from Moholy, adding that by that time he as a student had exhausted every possibility of compromise, which the New Bauhaus had represented. "I had successfully managed to be in schools for three years up to that point without ever getting anywhere near any sort of degree. I knew a lot of German, a lot of mathematics, and had a lot of experience. But finally at that point I think my family also realized that they had run out of coercion."

P A R T   I I I

Fritz tells Irving how Moholy Nagy isolated himself more and more by his opposition to Wright and Hofmann, saying that if "he had been a little less dogmatic and a little wiser, which I understand he became later, he would have known how to have dealt creatively with the situation, as Albers later did at Black Mountain."

> [At Black Mountain] they understood the difference—that change from Europe to the United States that Hofmann had also made. That this whole formalistic school was not going to work here, and this rigid base of semantics as being the philosophy of the Bauhaus—that everything can be understood and explained—which we all know can't be.
>
> One of the things with Hans that was so good for his students and people around him was his personal honesty and his always insisting that it come out of an experience—that everything had to be experienced. You see this again is that contradiction to the Bauhaus system which is superimposed on any—or which can be superimposed on any talent, any sort of experience—a system rather than a discipline, I would say. And Hans had a totally open mind. What he objected to [were] people who arrived at total abstraction and non-objectivity (which were separate categories in those days), without any visible means of experience. He really liked to know someone's way to a thing, how you arrived at this—and not intellectually—it was how you arrived painting-wise at any point.

Irving brings up Hofmann's relationship with Kandinsky.

> He loved the early paintings. He did not like the Bauhaus paintings. He was enormously suspicious of the intellectual aspects and systemization of the Bauhaus. And he felt that Kandinsky had suffered tremendously, but just *tremendously*, in being exposed to that atmosphere. It was really the whole thing at the Bauhaus that architecture was the prime art to which everything else was subordinate. And Hans just feeling "No, *painting* is that important. I'm not going to subordinate myself to anyone." This was his attitude straight on through.

Fritz mentions various other Hofmann students around him in New York at that time, 1938-40: George and Dora McNeil, Anne Ryan, Lee Krasner, Gerry Kamrowski, Perle Fine, Alan Leeper, Frances Field, Betty Paine, Igor Pantuhoff, Bob DeNiro (a little later), and Peggy Huck. He says that Wilfred Zogbaum was around all the time too (though he didn't attend the school), and Giorgio Cavallon and Mercedes Matter (who were no longer students), nevertheless remained close to Hofmann.

> I think this whole period of the thirties is one of the most misunderstood periods in American history. People just don't realize how lively it was. It wasn't so much that the school was a place where you learned, as where you were exposed to other people and their way of thinking. Hans really remained so far in the background as

possible. I would say his teaching was minimal, and by having no set discipline he really was able to bring out a great deal of self-discipline in people, making everyone responsible. Also it was not so much that people came to learn something, but to be in an atmosphere.

Fritz tells Irving about George McNeil working in a huge studio with Igor Pantuhoff (so huge that Igor had been able to hang one of de Kooning's large public murals in it) when McNeil was working on a very large mural himself, one that Fritz says "went through marvelous, marvelous transmutation because the picture changed constantly."

You know everybody was really aware of the value of other painters at that point. There was no isolation. I was still under twenty because I was born in 1919 and when I first met all of these people they seemed like marvelous figures because here was finally in really full blossom a world that I had always wanted to know. These people were all very connected because Lee Krasner was then living with the Rosenbergs, and there was a great deal of argument going on.

A lot of people actually weren't in the school but they would come to lectures. Gorky would come. In those years Hans's hearing was a little better and he tried to have formal lectures and he did so up on the Cape in the summer, I remember. These were open to the public and a great number of painters came. And they were full of life, full of argument. I remember a whole long, long argument that Hans and Gorky had concerning that Picasso still life, T H E   R E D   T A B L E C L O T H , about how Picasso had used certain ways of abstraction. Gorky brought out that Picasso had used the grapes on the tablecloth and the head in certain ways as a visual pun, and in that Gorky was already tending toward Surrealism. Hans maintained that they were purely painterly devices. I mean their positions were very clear. People discussed things like that at that time.

Irving asks Fritz what he felt he got most from the school.

I'd say equilibrium. I would say that's what he had to give: a sense of what painting could and could not do, a great sense of the potentials of painting—that's the word—that painting had in it many potentials. And that there was not that great a difference from Matisse to Miro, to Arp, to the Expressionists, to Kandinsky, that it could not be bridged.

There was always a double edge because Surrealism via Dali had taken New York in a great storm at that particular point. And I would say that Hans felt his own position to be half-way between the constructive Bauhaus-type camp and the Surrealist total commitment to magic realism. One of his great favorites, besides Matisse, was Miro. He loved Miro's painting. He had already at that time a Miro watercolor and then in 1938 Miz Hofmann brought over a big Miro for them. Hans liked the work of other painters. He did not have any sense of exclusivity. He liked a great range of work. He liked very conservative, almost academic painters.

Irving asks whether Hofmann liked Dali's paintings.

No. Dali was really a *bete noire*. [Hofmann] liked his antics, but he hated his paintings. He really hated those paintings. But he liked his antics because he felt they were sort of marvelous and liberating for the United States. Which they were. Dali really represented Surrealism. You see, Hans and the Bauhaus, Albers, all of that group were the first of the 'thirties refugees from Hitler. Then came the war and we got the whole second wave of all the Surrealist painters—two separate and overlapping influences. Because Gorky was already here. He had developed here, [as had] Bill de Kooning, long before the second influx arrived. And [John] Graham. These were all independent people that had come to this country. And [Frederick] Kiesler was already here at that point. They represented really important figures around whom groups arranged themselves and dissolved. Gorky taught in those years. He had a lot of private students. Leger and Dali were visitors, birds of passage at that point. Leger hadn't come here to settle and Dali was doing all kinds of strange things—the [storefront] windows and public manifestations.

Fritz makes the point that with the coming of the war [and this second wave of émigrés] the kind of exhibitions seen in New York changed. "Instead of imported shows of Picasso, [the dealers] became much more involved in actual work being produced here. This was the first time that [we] became aware of [André] Masson, for example. Strangely enough this country had a tremendously tonic effect on him, because for a very short while during the time he was here he produced the few paintings that really stand as his best work."

And then the great thing to see was Mondrian. I mean Mondrian had been an isolated figure until 1939, and then suddenly there was this embarrassment of riches. Mondrian had one or two pictures that you would see and finally that one-man show at the Valentine Gallery where it was a marvelous revelation. You began to see his work in depth and its impact was very strong.

Fritz describes the frequent evening meals at Rocco's behind the Mills Hotel and the lengthy arguments that took place there.

I remember a really big argument about Matta. Lee Krasner was always vociferous and she always had a great liveliness about her, and a great "this is right and this is wrong." She had a very strong moral basis on which she judged things, and when the first Matta show took place she was really outraged at the unpaintedness of it, at its illusionistic quality.

Fritz mentions that the home of Herbert and Mercedes Matter was another meeting place for a great many of the painters, native and émigré. Alexander Calder staged a performance of his Circus at one of their "evenings."

Leger would visit them quite often. He was a very approachable man. He really enjoyed the New York scene. He liked to go to movies. And that's where we spent a great deal of time in those days—going to double features. But it was so casual and people placed so little... No one was interested in history then. That is one thing I would say is the main change from then to now.

Fritz met John Graham at this point and remained in touch with him throughout Graham's life. Graham was Hilla Rebay's secretary at the Museum of Non-Objective Art (later the Guggenheim Museum), and had just published, *System and Dialectics of Art*, a book Fritz and Hofmann both admired. Fritz mentions to Irving that in later years, when Graham had turned against Picasso, he regretted the praise he had heaped upon in him in the book. Many people were shocked by Graham's sudden attack on Picasso, but Fritz sensed a general feeling of disappointment with Picasso after the war.

The thing is that everybody had expected the war to be as vital a stimulus to Picasso as the Spanish Civil War had been, because the last pictures that we had all seen were the G U E R N I C A and the girl with the chicken. After that everything seemed soft, didn't seem to have the... And there was a terrible, a general letdown that this had happened in this particular way after the war. I mean, I think this was not only true of John Graham; it was true of about nine-tenths of the painters.

After the war many American painters generalized anti-French attitudes from what they perceived as Picasso's failure to maintain a high level of artistry. Fritz and Hofmann remained steadfastly international in their outlook, however, and in 1950 they organized an exhibition at the Provincetown Art Association to counter an anti-European tendency: "Young Painters in U.S. and France." They issued a joint manifesto of sorts to accompany the show, called "Against Ostrich Politics in the Arts." Student and teacher now worked in common cause as Fritz explains:

The whole thing was that Hans hated nationalism...and regionalism. He didn't like "isms" at all. He liked the human being, the human personality, the human commitment. He saw clearly that certain deficiencies were taking place, but he always felt that art in our time was essentially an international matter, not a regional or a national one.

SELECTIONS FROM
THE ARTIST'S NOTEBOOKS

Selected by Robert Lawlor

INTRODUCTION

The following quotations have been compiled from Fritz Bultman's notebooks with entries taken over three decades from the 1940's to the 1970's. They are arranged into four sections each containing three terms that represent the key ideas and motivations behind Bultman's art.

The first section: form, space and surface are the three most fundamental elements of the visually perceived world. Bultman considered them the most reduced and objective base of visual reality and the pure compositional ground of every work of art.

The second section: image, transparency and symbol are the means by which the subjective mind embellishes or builds identity, meaning and value upon and within the pure visual world of space and form.

The third section: plasticity, ambiguity and paradox are the painter's tools or modus operandi through which the artist fuses together the visual and inner experience in a single creation.

The fourth section: life, the body and art are the sources and generators of the process of creation. Each reflecting and fertilizing the other.

The contemplation of these four groups of terms, like the recurrent forms in Bultman's work, filled the entirety of his life and his art. He found that the implications of these ideas wove together vast worlds of human experience from the psychological to the metaphysical, from the spiritual to the embodied, from myth to the mundane. Rarely does one find an artist's work in which the fidelity to purely visual principles has resulted in such an encompassing synthesis of our existence.

1.   The picture, the plastic means, for me seems to be moving again. I am involved in contours and the possibility of a painting being conceived as totally positive. Each shape is full. Each division cuts off a piece that is complete and total. But the whole is spatial and full. Until now this seemed to be possible only with a geometric straight line or, if curves are used, then regular forms. I believe that a free form, an organic form can, or more naturally must, assume this same positive fullness. All painting until now has relied on cubist or precubist recession of forms into space. I sense the retina as full and the painting must be full with the unmeasured coincidences of vision. Everything on earth is full of life and death, only in the void of outer space is there receding recessive space.

2.   We want the flatness of the canvas to be reconstituted but with the space of the stars. We want an enormous volume constituted of the interlacing of positive and negative but reconstituted in two dimensions. The plane is an actual part of the whole canvas. Once the artist worked toward the creation of two dimensionality out of the object and surrounding space (this is a fundamental difference between the plastic of the early years of this century and today). Today we accept and start with the two dimensional and work toward the creation of plastic space. These means are in themselves neutral but again even the means can be changed with the metaphysic of the individual artist—involving the means in the dialogue with subjective matter.

3.   Historically the modern revival of plastics had to do with the desire for the integrity of the canvas—its two dimensional aspect. This grew in importance from impressionism on—Seurat used it to give solidity and architecture to his compositions—to give them the form that Impressionism is accused of deserting. Cezanne and then the Cubists pushed it back further with the organization and ordering of space. The original purpose of this movement being the re-establishment of the surface to recreate the original surface. In a sense, its function was like baptism; to establish an a priori innocence. Mondrian achieved this and for this reason, in the thirties, Mondrian was considered the logical end of painting. The Bauhaus canonized him with the laurel that henceforth painting would be absorbed into architecture. Alas painting and its plastic development is not amenable to prophets and prediction. In the immediate past Pollock defined one movement of dealing with the quality of surface; the ultimate eccentric pushing against the edges. Another has been the reintroduction of symmetrical shaped canvases from Romanesque painting and more recently shapes that are amorphous. These movements in different ways challenge the idea that the vitality of the plastic impulse is over. Then there is the other aspect—accepting the two dimensional as obvious. Plasticism has been introduced to create space and spaciousness in order to obviate the claustrophobia of what would remain—design.

IMAGE, TRANSPARENCY AND SYMBOL

1.   Representation is not only depiction, nor is metaphor the only "out". There is what I call transparency—images are glimpsed through images. Today more than ever a single image does not suffice. It is this frustration with singleness that pushes my work beyond not just to a more complex or simple resolution but a resolution that carries more aspects of the transparency of the object/subject relationships in which I find myself constantly involved.

2.   Experience is essentially sensuous, emotional, non-verbal, needing another medium in order to communicate, to express or to clarify. The medium carries meaning because as soon as experience begins to be collected and made permanent it operates on many other levels. This is so because essentially experience is transparent. By that I mean as soon as I begin to draw, say a figure, I am sensuously aware simultaneously of that figure as a person as colour, as a volume within a volume of space, as a volume composed of separate volumes, as a harmonious whole. I am aware that the living in me is purely and totally real and subjective. As objectively as I try to put down what I see, I see it through me. I cannot abdicate even if I have taken a position to the right or left of the figure. I must deal with these two realities. This figure I have seen or felt, my own included. In this moment when I put pencil to paper, I perpetuate what is experienced as an array of contradictions and paradox. These paradox are set in motion by the conflicting demands of realities in the creation of a new reality. The shifting sensations of each artist of time and space make each apprehension a unique experience. As I have drawn, these conflicting realities each proclaim their paramountcy in succession.

3.   Cool breeze, the Dog has set—and suddenly there is a chill wind—Goat Pan is dead—the tent of summer is still spread wide; another 40 days—but the fierce fingers of summer relax into a loving hand—salad will grow again and we will hear the locust and the dawn breeze will be cool—the golden children of summer beaches. Pan escapes from classrooms and their golden stomachs will forget the sun that they now rival—How long will the seas stay warm and curve to the slow furrowing of its surface? That surface that carries me weightless but moving—exhaling where it joins the the sky. Actaeon's remains are eaten by the cutworms and the golden spiders, by the nosy small animal looking for burrows by the many small tasks before the sun sets due west—Actaeon's dogs, unleashed and masterless, have gone beyond the seas and now the Scorpion begins to reign in heaven. The exhaltations of earth last till noon; it is a sound until the cool breeze and the cool water and the cool land marry into blueness.

4.   The female and the pillar of fire. The prismic quality of the Trinity recurrent—interchangeable, leaves for flame, hair for flame. The symbol of the trinity carried by the female—a double meaning the furred sexual female—ovoid, ovary as the bearer of the

prismic, the shifting or rather variable spirit. It is in a way a complete symbol of the duality of man, of his might and his clarification. It is near to the eye within the triangle of the Freemasons but here the clarification contains the night. The symbol of the triangle is one of infinite variety, of possibility contained yet capable of sustaining interior and exterior forces. The form shifts but never changes.

5.   Persephone, born of earth, of day, wheat fields and cornflower is the inner spirit of life, rather than the inquisitive Psyche. The temporal quality of Persephone the spirit and the seasons; she is Ceres in the cave. In a Pompeian fresco, only Ceres' back is revealed and a sheath of wheat and flowers. This spirit is rather ravished by night and submits only to part of the nuptial Bacchanale. The world today is essentially Swinburne's Garden of Paradise: the fertility God is not dead but lost in lament. The pomegranate is only a taste of the dark garden.

6.   The boats, the carriers of men—they are the symbol of the mother, the confinement, a limitation of life like in the womb. The prows are arched like the full stomach of carrying mothers. The sensation that one hates to disembark, they are complete microcosms. When one thinks of galleys there is a memory of centipedes pregnant with humanity. The ocean is the mother of all life. The boat becomes the temporary womb. The throbbing of the engines the pulsation of the blood. On the ship in the womb, the wanderer can reconstitute his life. The safeness and lack of complexity allow the natural instincts to return in their correct order. The ship absorbs the fears and anxieties of the land that holds the wanderer in a frozen trance, and here the wanderer can feel the heritage, his position as leader, as the son of a king. But only by placing his crown in the belly of the whale will he know his kingdom. Deeper in the body, the wanderer nursed, suckled, slowly changing to his blood memory of things in the arms of the mother, our mermaid. The poetry of an abandoned boat. On land the wanderer becomes the martyred arrow-pierced St. Sebastian whose eye is never closed. No rest, nothing escapes these senses of perception. The eye that never closes, the ear that hears the constant accusations.

7.   When I was a child the speed of Plato's chariot of black horses, their nostrils breathing fire, made a terrific impression. They are the symbol of spiritual death and regeneration with perhaps more of this quality than the Christ or Osiris myth although all are linked. For the artist these recurrent images like the stages of insanity induce states of creative hysteria. The quality of seizing on a theme and using it as a ladder—the sense of exhilaration that I felt with my fevers and the desire for exhaustion (to exhaust myself) of this extension into oblivion. The blackness of night, the lack of dreams, Plato being carried away by horses—this is the underworld.

PLASTICITY, AMBIGUITY AND PARADOX

1.   To experience the no with the yes, the negative with the positive, is essentially the plastic aspect of living. To extend to its maximum, the tension between opposites is perhaps a fair meaning of plastic.

2.   At this moment a question arises which I am really defining. In drawing does not everything exist by the definition of others? And does not this ambiguity define a function of drawing? Are we not experiencing the space through the object existing in it? This paradox of two and three dimensions, is the center of plastic concepts. Plastic defines itself as the experience of and creation of three dimensions in two and in reverse the ability to sense a space through implication and relationship. The plastic is the awareness of the reality of the medium.

3.   The plastic is neither a style nor a method but rather a goal in which everything tries to become clear and all the pieces fall in the internal dialogue of painting. It is painting defining itself in its own terms of form, space, transparency, etc. Terms that are blunted when spoken but very clear when seen. Again like magic the public sees the results but the way, the means have obscured themselves during the act. All the means are in themselves neutral and remain so unless given utterance with precision and force and coerced into a work of art which means subjected to the subject of the artist, a vision.

4.   We have only touched the possibility of disassociation within the idea of the plastic...much the same way that the possibilities and range of abstraction, and the possibilities of non-figuration, have only been touched upon. One must realize that development is not a straight forward development. A start is made. Then nothing. Then another start. Contradiction then quiet. Then branches into other directions. Thus plastic can mean taking any material and disciplining it into constructional means of art. Primarily the means to construct light and space. Not to imitate, not to approximate, not to fool the eye, not to substitute but to build another dimension. Thus no matter how banal the use, these means of themselves *are* metaphor. Piling up feces, fountains of blood, the exhibiting of a nude body on a silver cross are the pathos of life itself—and after the moment of surprise and outrage one is alone with the daily paper. That eerie other life that persistent presence, that is art, just hasn't been evoked, hasn't been created, hasn't been built.

5.   This plastic awareness has been taken for granted, been dismissed, been rediscovered—its history parallels the so called history of art because it is enormously expansive and because it has been present, in some form, in all visual art. It is itself a continuous and comprehensive whole.

6.   Experience of paradox is central to the art of art—simultaneously the space of the stars and the flatness of a piece of paper, the way up and the way down are the same way. In sculpture it has to do with the levitation of mass—by displacement, to make inert mass float and even soar. In colour it has to do with converting paint to light and to transform the specific intention of the artist; to make red tender and blue vicious to make yellow passive. To attempt—rather to tempt reason. Even in architecture room exists—space has to be created. Here by scale, there by the interruption of continuity—the space is made active and functional.

7.   We know nothing about our art—it is a paradox. With our language we really understand nothing concrete about it—it is all relational ie. the relation of space to colour—of colour making volume, of colour making light, of light being related to space—of all colour being colour only in a relational way.

LIFE, THE BODY AND ART

1.   The human body may be seen as a vessel of energy or as a history of the past that presents itself in the present moment of fruition. The female body like the horse has meaning associated with it beyond any we can consciously project or imagine. The vase quality of the female body was the first that forced itself into my conscious mind and then the wave meander then the ropeness of the twisted torso and arms in space. Now I see a knot that sometimes the hips, thighs and legs create. Drawing the body is tonic for me.

2.   Sometimes we hide this subject/object from ourselves in order to explore possibilities, before jelling our sensations into a single vision. Sometimes it is left dangling as a possibility. For me the human body is the center of everything—of bodily sensations—of observation (I would rather look at people than art or landscape). I love to draw women, their beauty is something both objective to look at and subjectively to wonder about. I really wonder about beautiful women, perhaps in the way Flaubert or Ingres did: Salambo and the Grande Odalisque. It is strange that all of Graham's women are clothed. I wonder about nudity, nakedness, *that* body.

3.   The desire to possess and to be are one; the curse of being an artist is being in the center—aware of the beauty of archetypes—Odalisque and the Warrior. But that sensation of the human body is manifold, I am, I feel, everything.

4.   Since I was a child I have felt that certain mysteries are contained (or embodied) by the human body. I notice that my grandson gives a special emphasis to nudity (perhaps there is something morbid about this preoccupation). However to the fresh imagination

there is something unexplainable by the nudity of the human body—by its roundness and fullness and sudden concavity. The idea of coming out of or issuing from another body is almost more than the human mind can grasp. It is almost as vague and incomprehensible as, at death, returning to earth. That the function of this body should be the continuity of life is perhaps its greatest mystery, because its mass has so developed as to be otherwise directed, and yet to forget its function is to be faced with extinction.

5.   It is the experience of transmutation, of growth and decline, of illumination, that the process of painting contains. Only by going through this process, by losing one's way, by mess, by total chaos, of ones own making, come unexpected results that one cannot anticipate in any other way. "It is all vague" Mr. Koestler says easily "You have to keep it vague and flexible otherwise you fall into the trap which Whitehead called misplaced concreteness. If you jump too quickly to a hypothesis, that is misplaced concreteness... leave it vague, fleeting, like water running down your hand". Through the act of painting the intention of the artist is revealed to himself.

6.   Recently while reading the manuscript of a friend's book—I was overwhelmed with the single dimension of action piled on action—moving in a single line, relentlessly in one direction. I found only one moment that gave such constancy a pause of otherness and I seized upon it like a branch breaking a fall. It is the one detail that remained clearest in mind from the entire fantastic fantasy of destruction. It stands as a small resting place for the mind contemplating chaos. When I finished reading my one reaction was: give this book more of this, so that it will have plastic dimension. This is what Mondrian meant when he said "I saw the tragic in a high cathedral or a wide horizon". The tragic of inequivalence. Life is equivalence.

7.   But in the end only that art that interests artists is alive. Today all art must protest art. It must affirm life and uniqueness of life the preciousness of life—by means that art is random and organic. However, great ages of art do not have to do with personal freedom. It is very hard to create in a world of regimentation, arbitrary, meaningless disciplined power. Power that is grey and denying. But even here there is paradox. Art is discipline—discipline that has no useful rational basis—It is self discipline and the artist in many ways is cut off from the movement toward freedom in his own time.

8.   Whatever is burning, inescapably real and important: whatever is the inevitable choice; whatever has to get onto the canvas, despite will, knowledge, taste and a hundred other obstacles—this is what makes the reality of the painted. This reality gives art its reason. It is perhaps the friction of all these realities, the painter, the means, the painted, each demanding attention—that brings the work to life.

FRITZ BULTMAN

illustrations

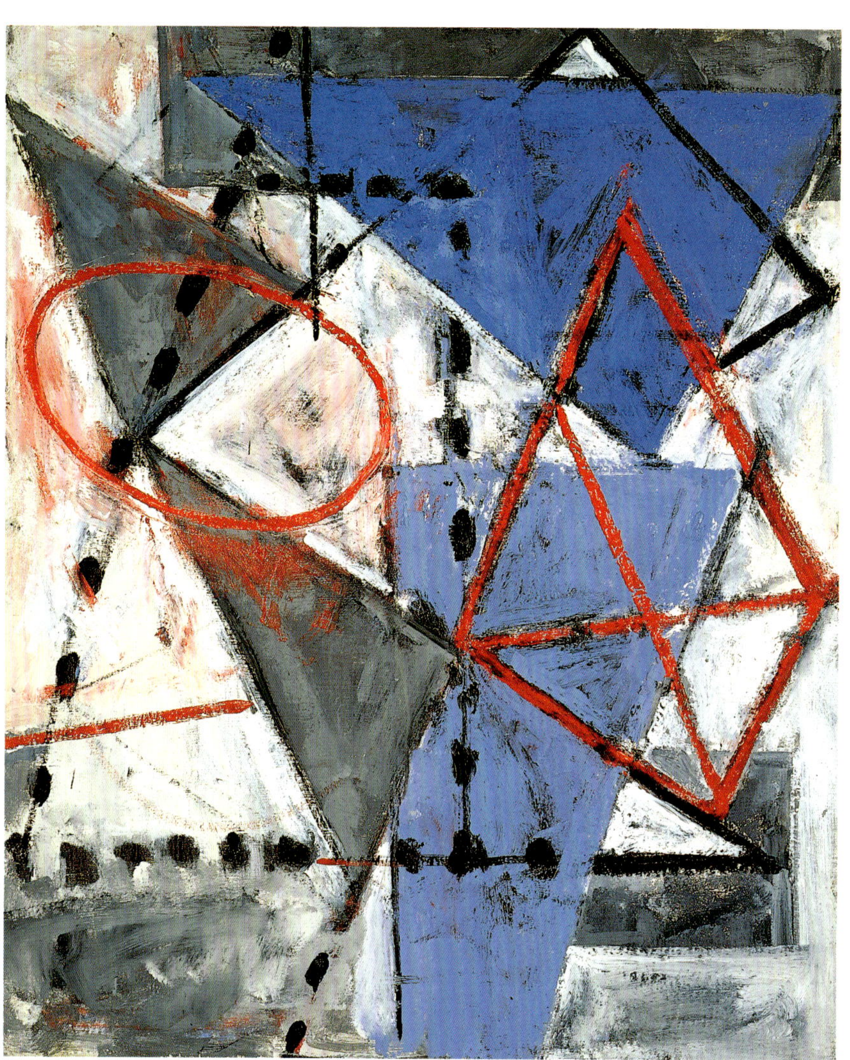

I

ACTEON MASK STILL LIFE

1941

oil on canvas

30 × 24

Lent by The Roger Houston Ogden Collection, New Orleans, Louisiana

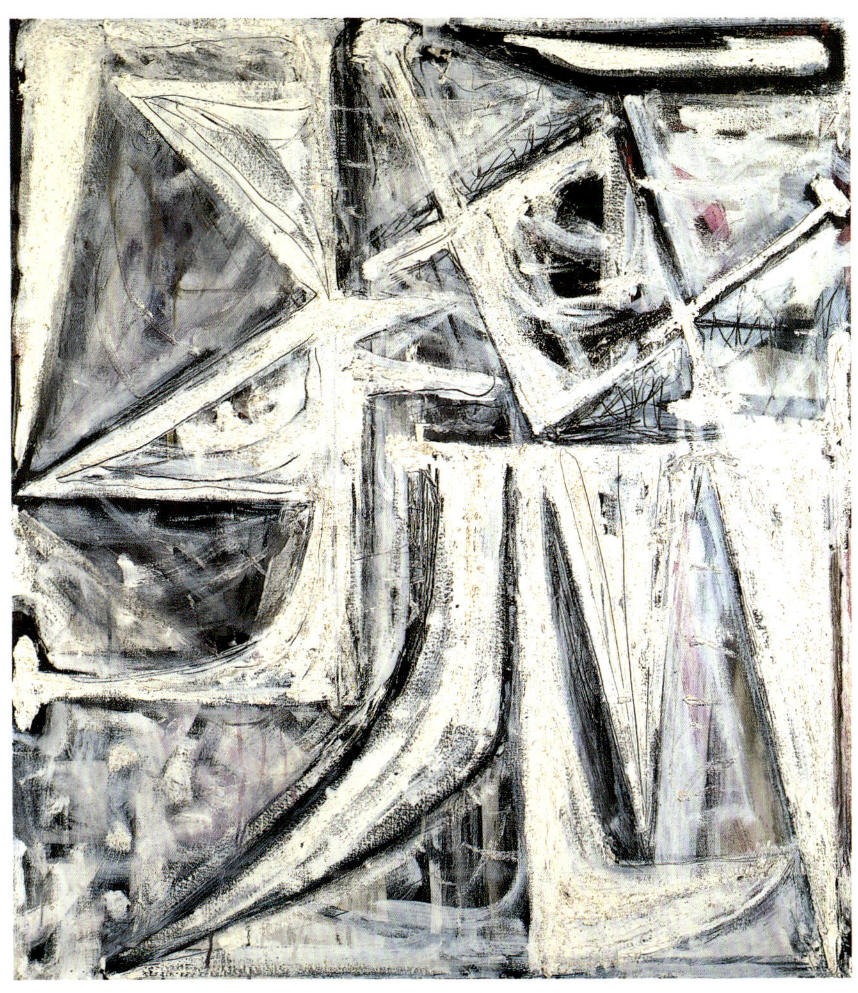

5

THE WHITE READER
1949
oil on canvas
40 × 36

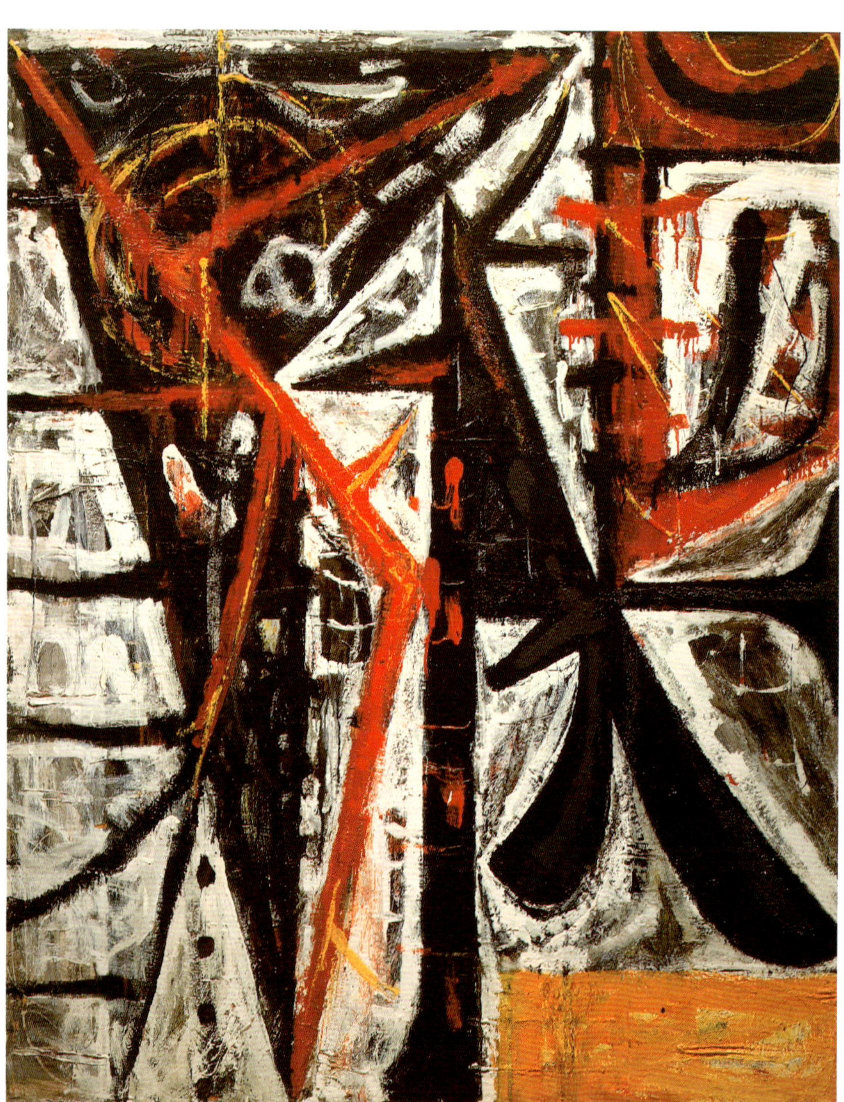

6

THE   HUNTER
1949
oil on celotex
60 × 48

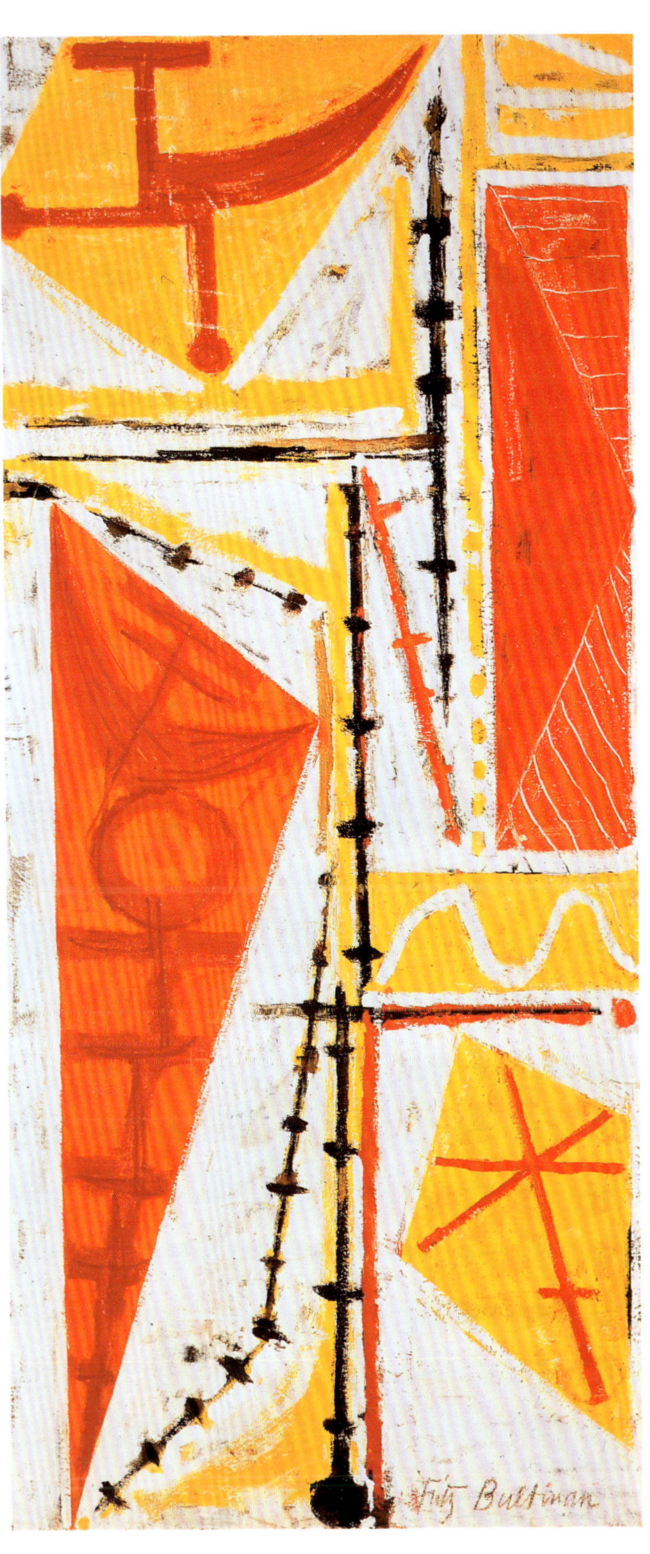

8

THE RED KING

1949

oil on celotex

64 × 28

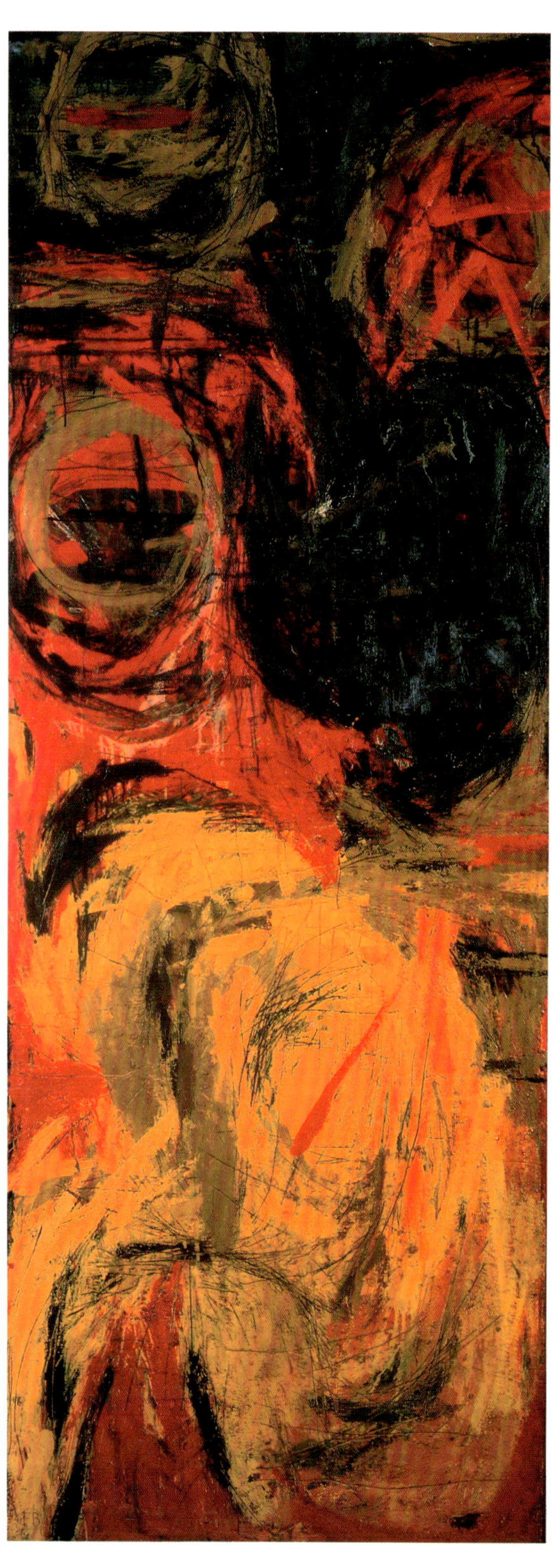

10

VIA PORTA ROMANA
1952
oil on masonite
96 × 36

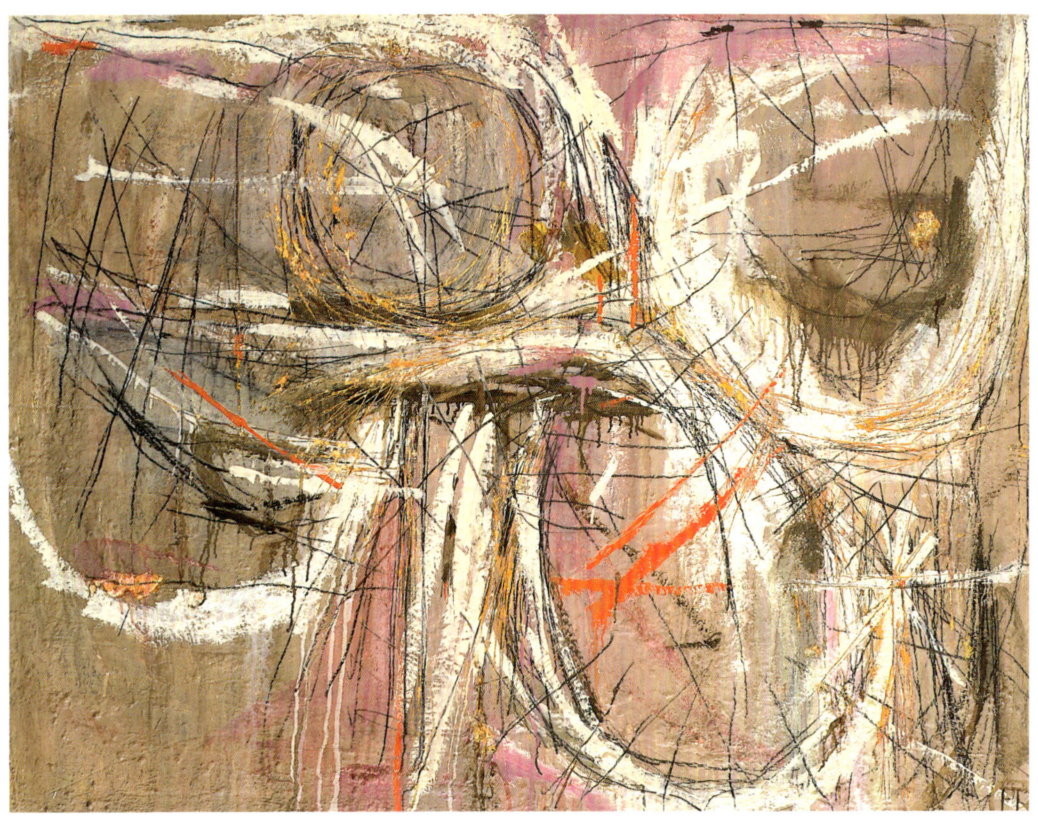

12

INTERIOR - RAIN
1953
oil on canvas
38 x 49 1/2

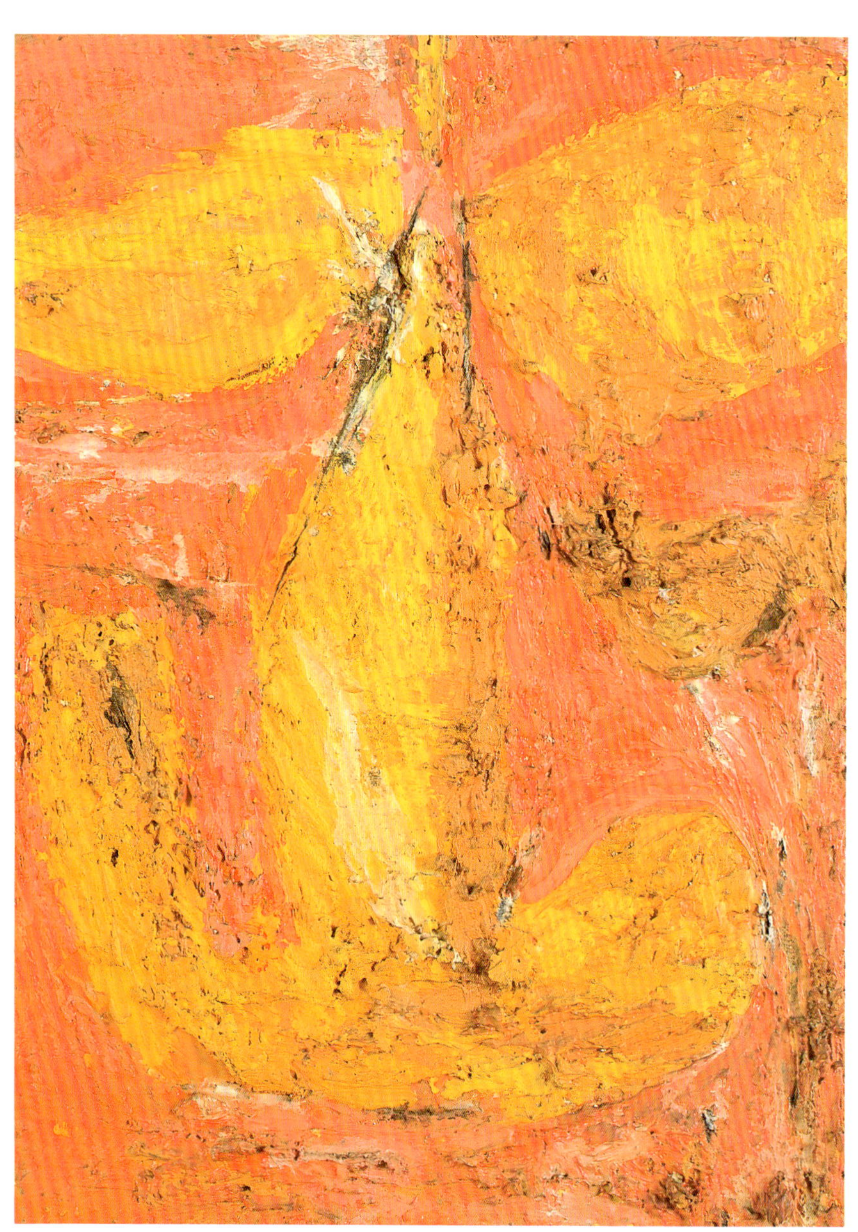

13

FROM THE DOOR
1954
oil on panel
14 x 10

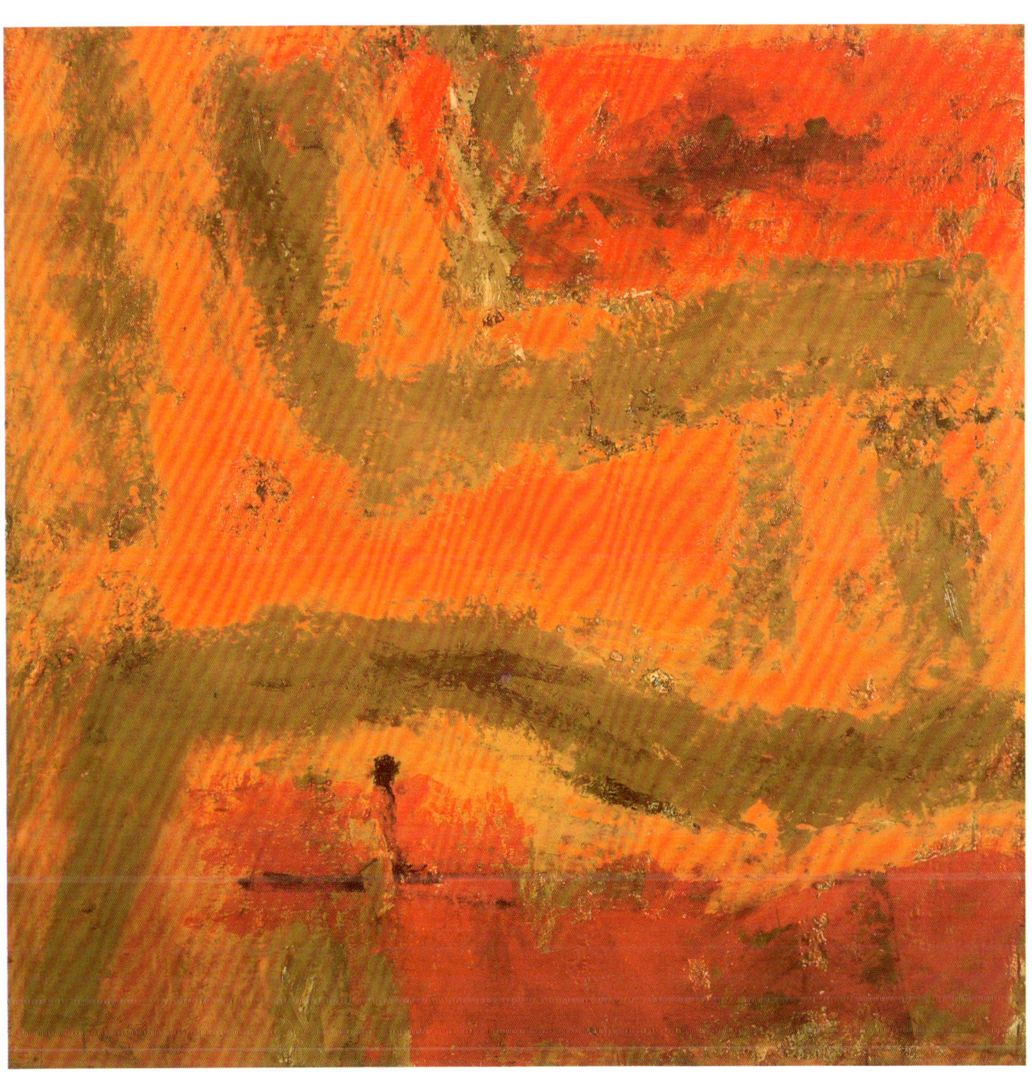

15

SKIN OF THE NEGRESS
1957
oil on canvas
48 × 48

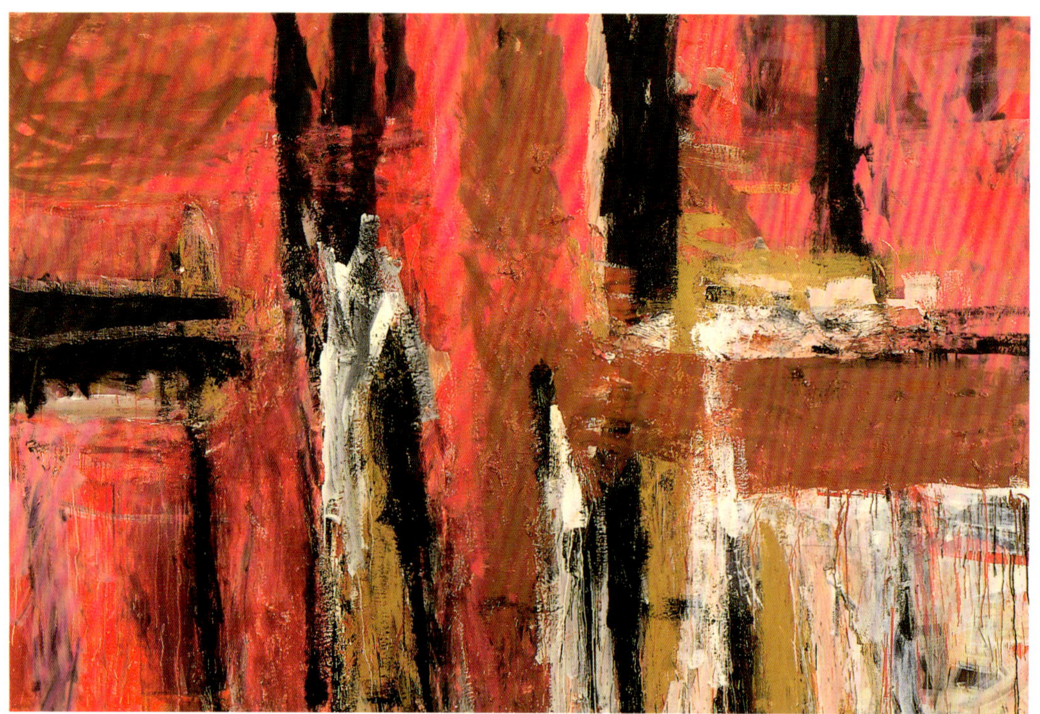

16

ROSA PARK
1958
oil on canvas
72 x 108

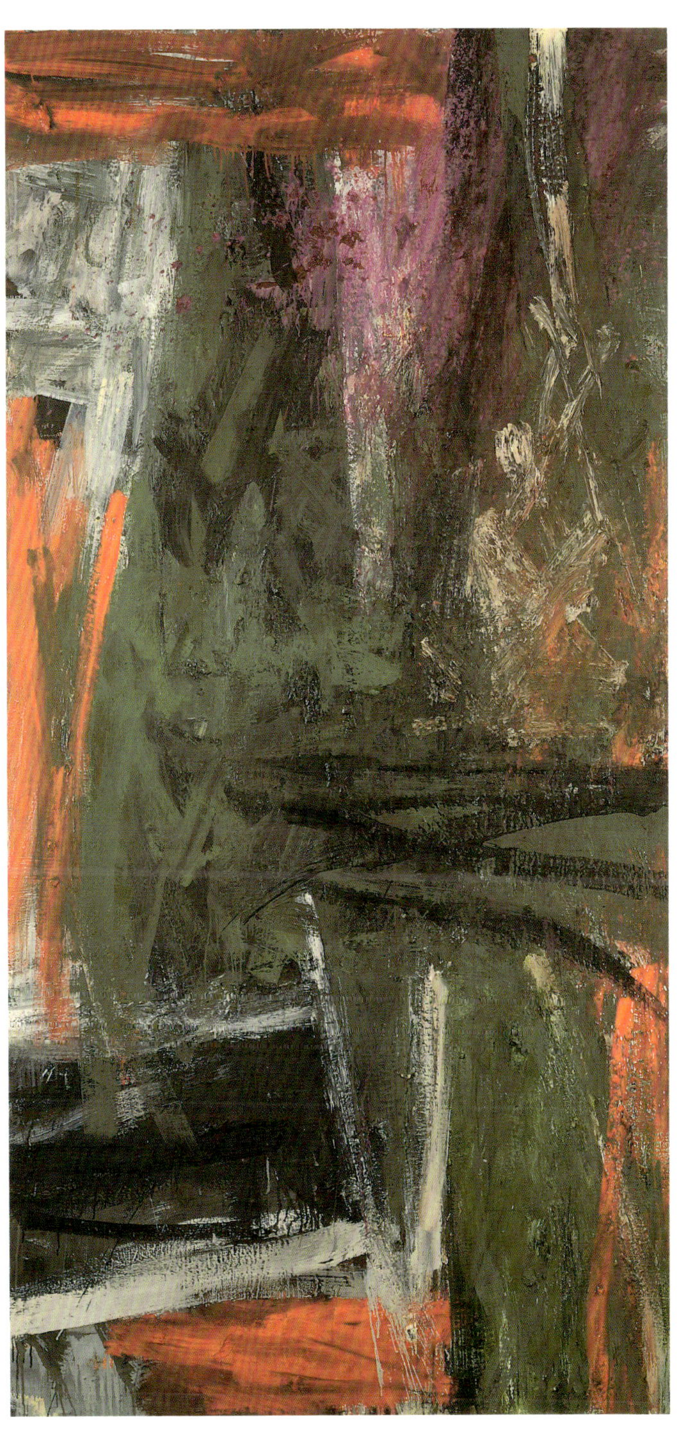

19

COOL GATE
1960
oil on canvas
96 x 48

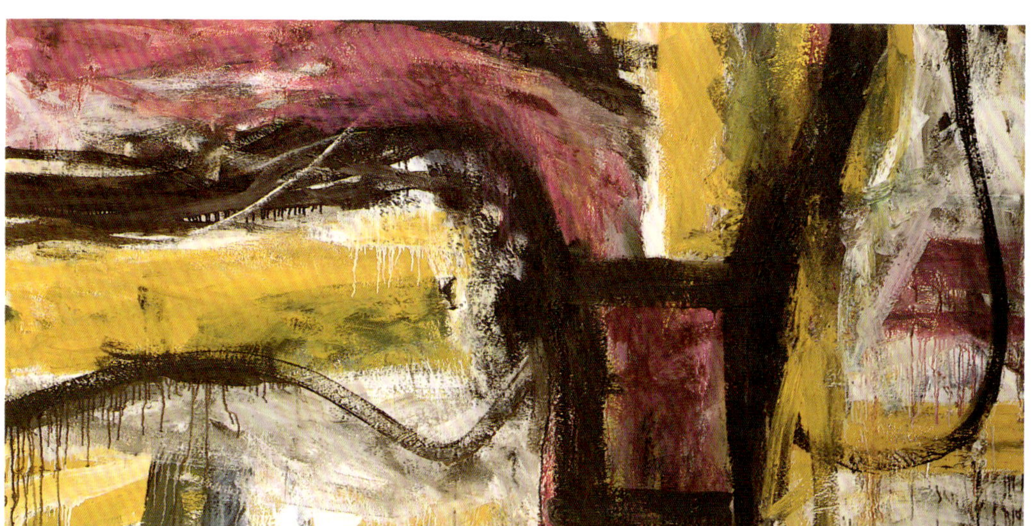

21

THIRD
1961
oil on canvas
48 × 96

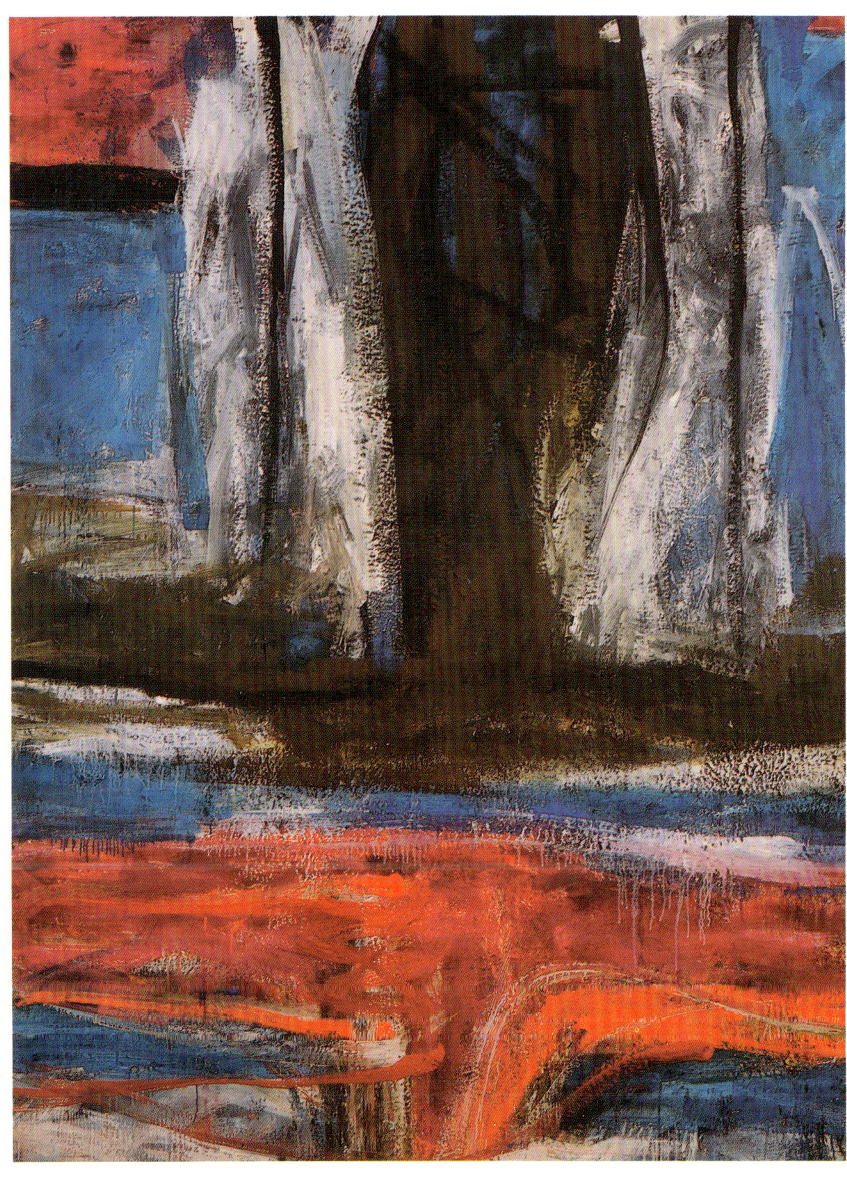

22

M OVER W
1961
oil on canvas
96 x 72

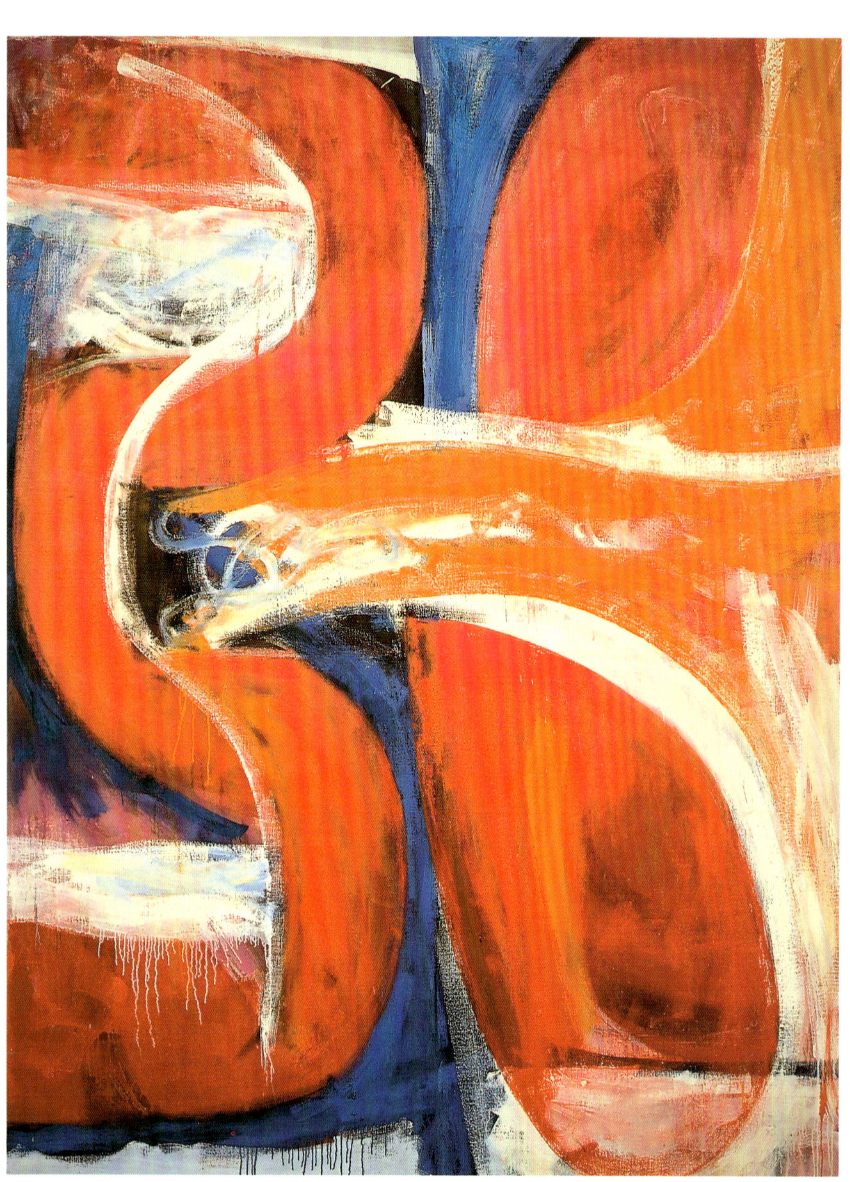

24

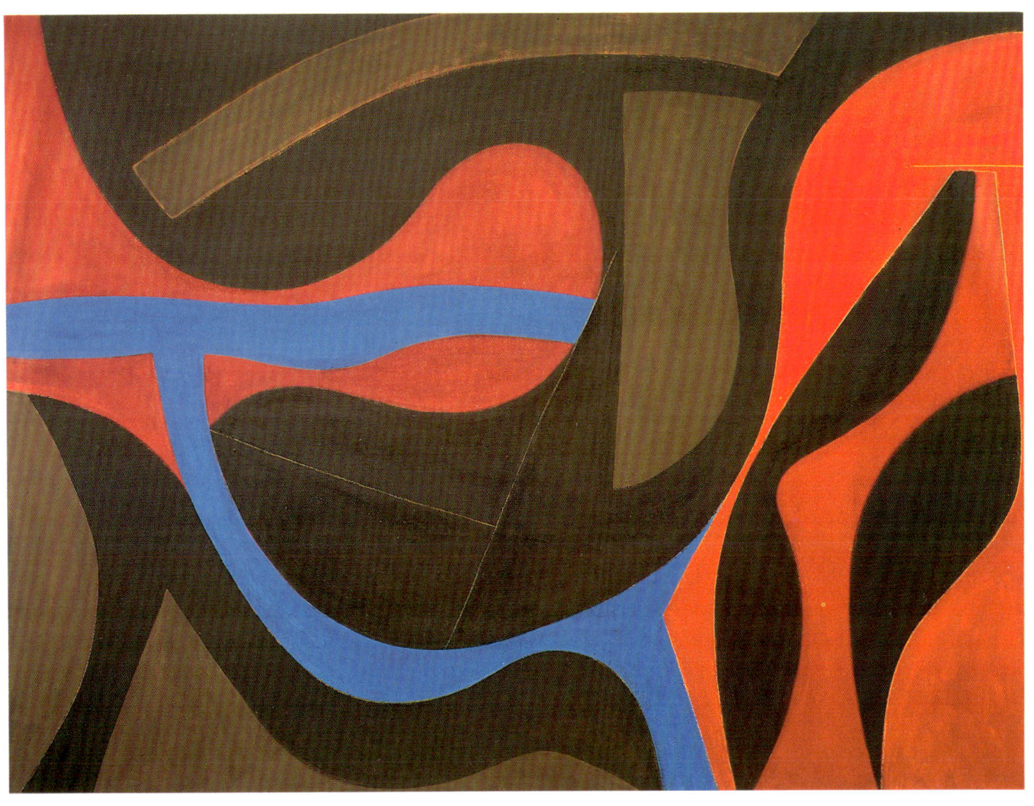

29

INTRUSION OF BLUE
1974
oil on canvas
72 x 96

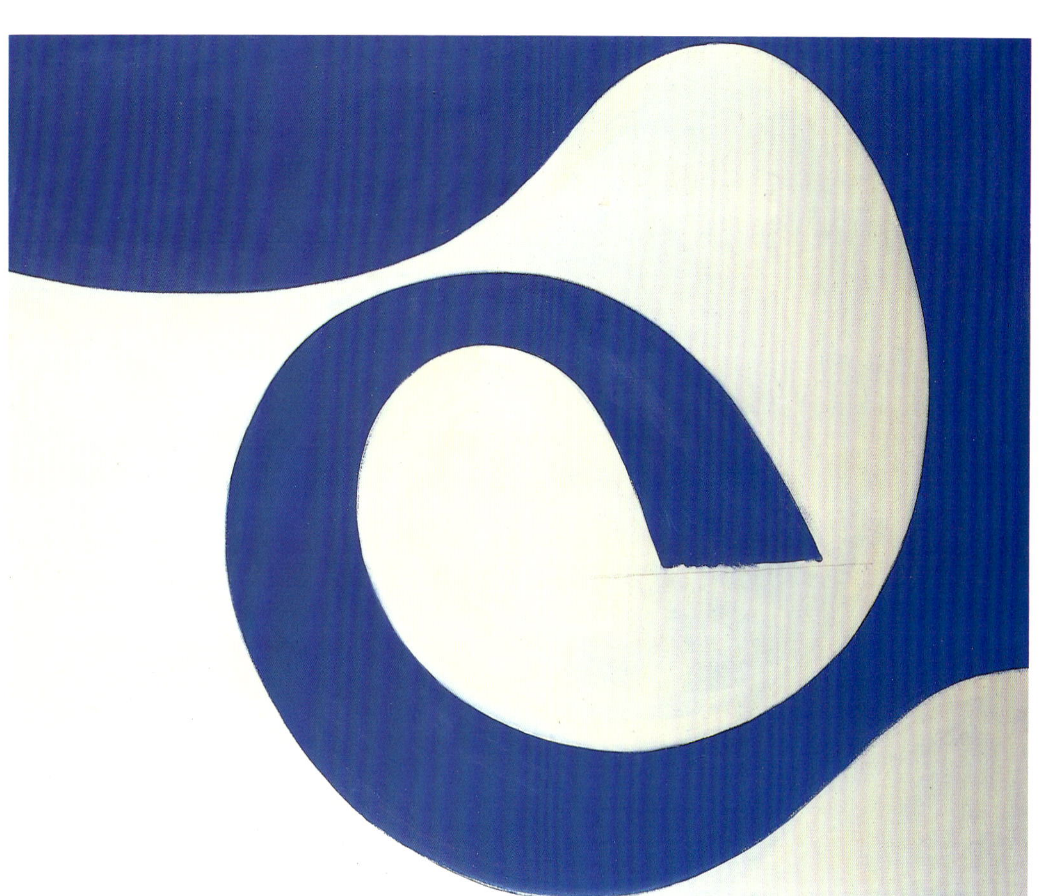

THE BLUE WAVE
1983
oil on canvas
48 × 58

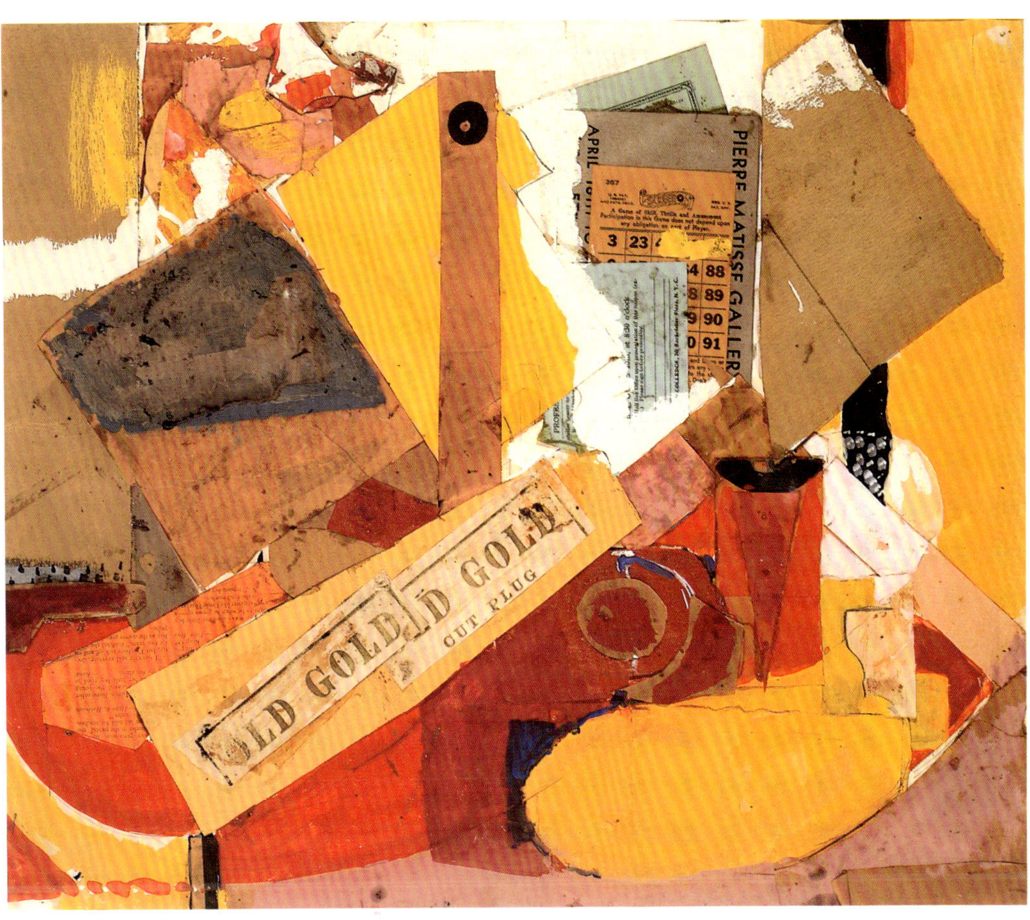

31

OLD GOLD

1938

collage of painted papers

19 1/2 × 22 3/4

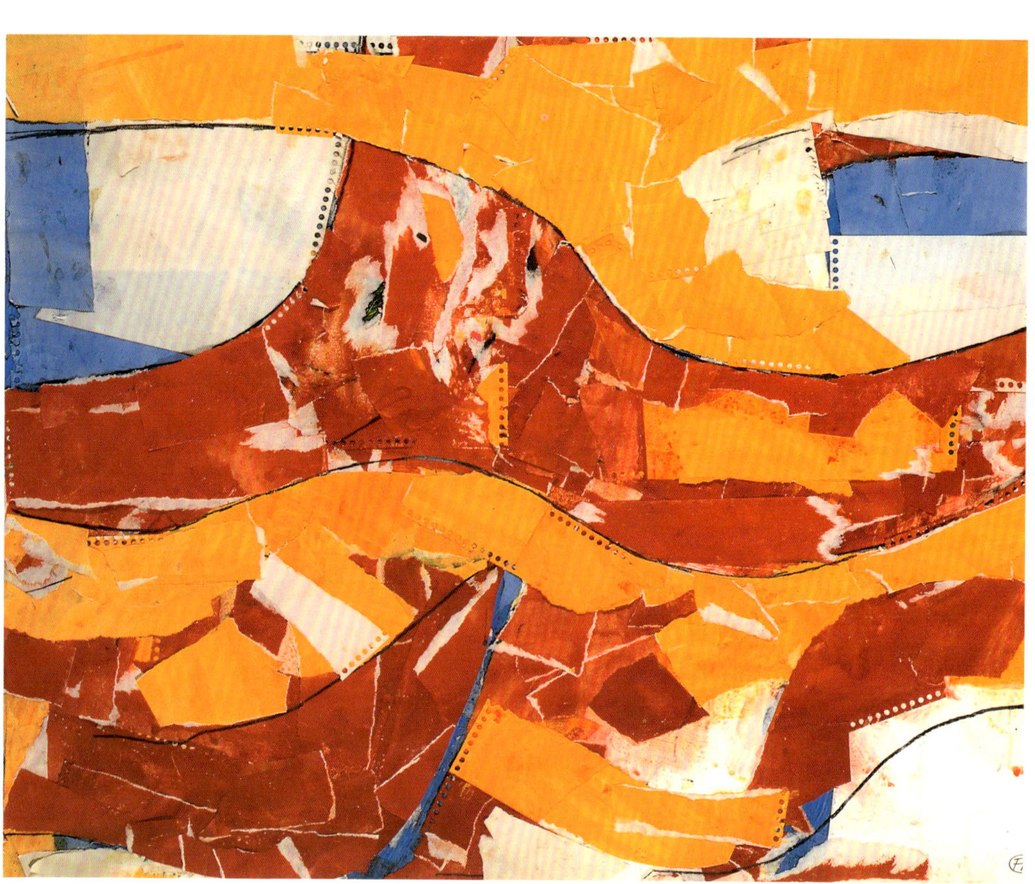

I L I U M

1966

collage of painted papers

23 × 29

Lent by Mrs. George P. Kramer, New York, New York

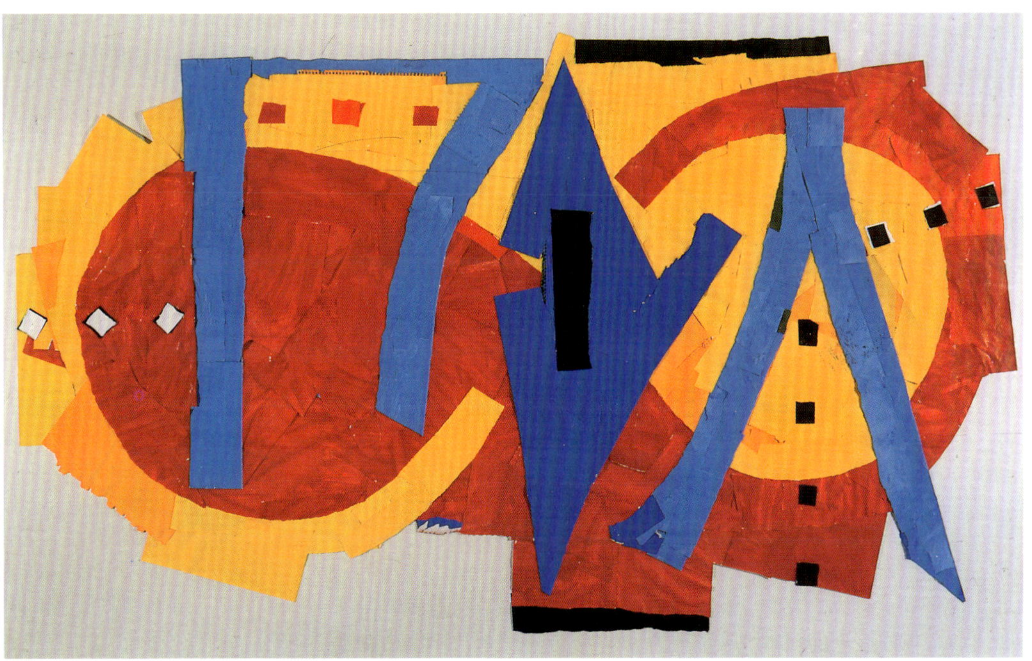

38

1975

collage of painted papers

48 × 78

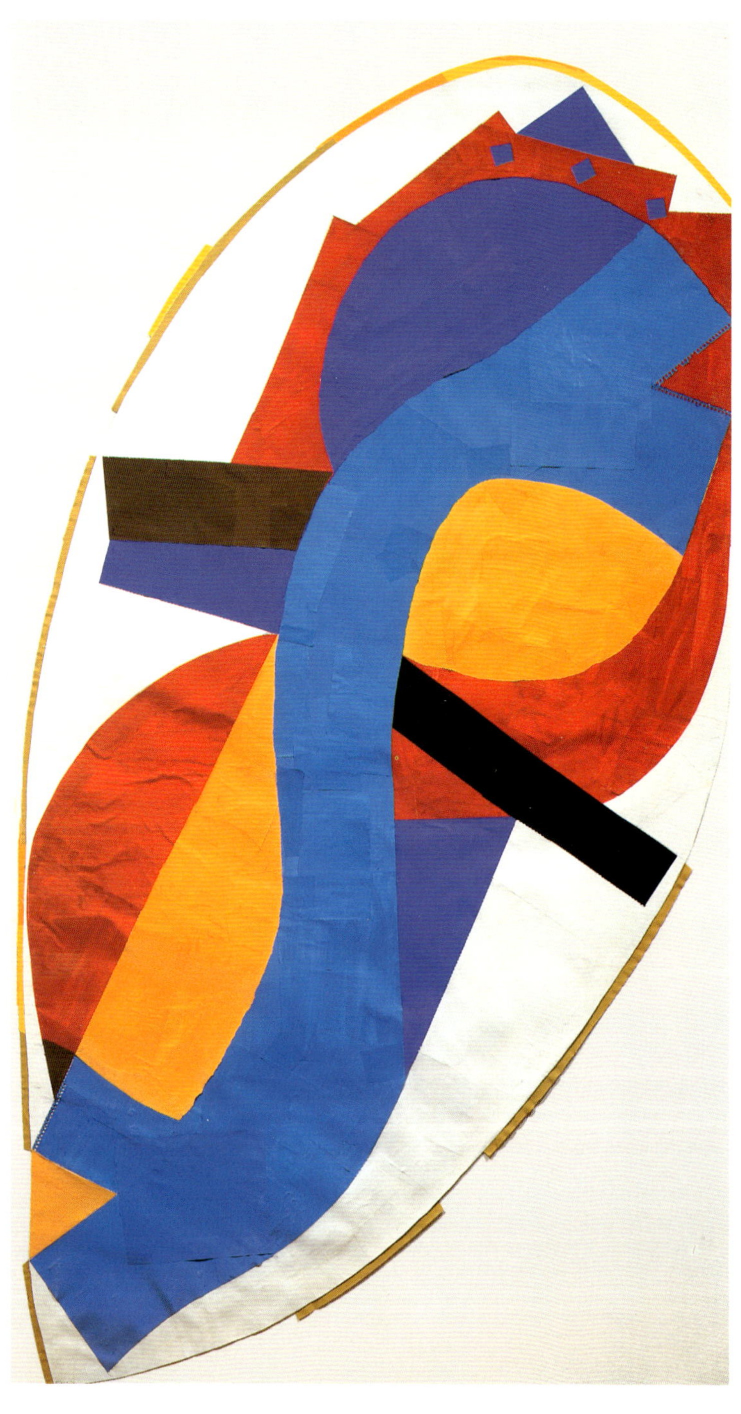

40

THE BEACH
1978
collage of painted papers
86 × 48

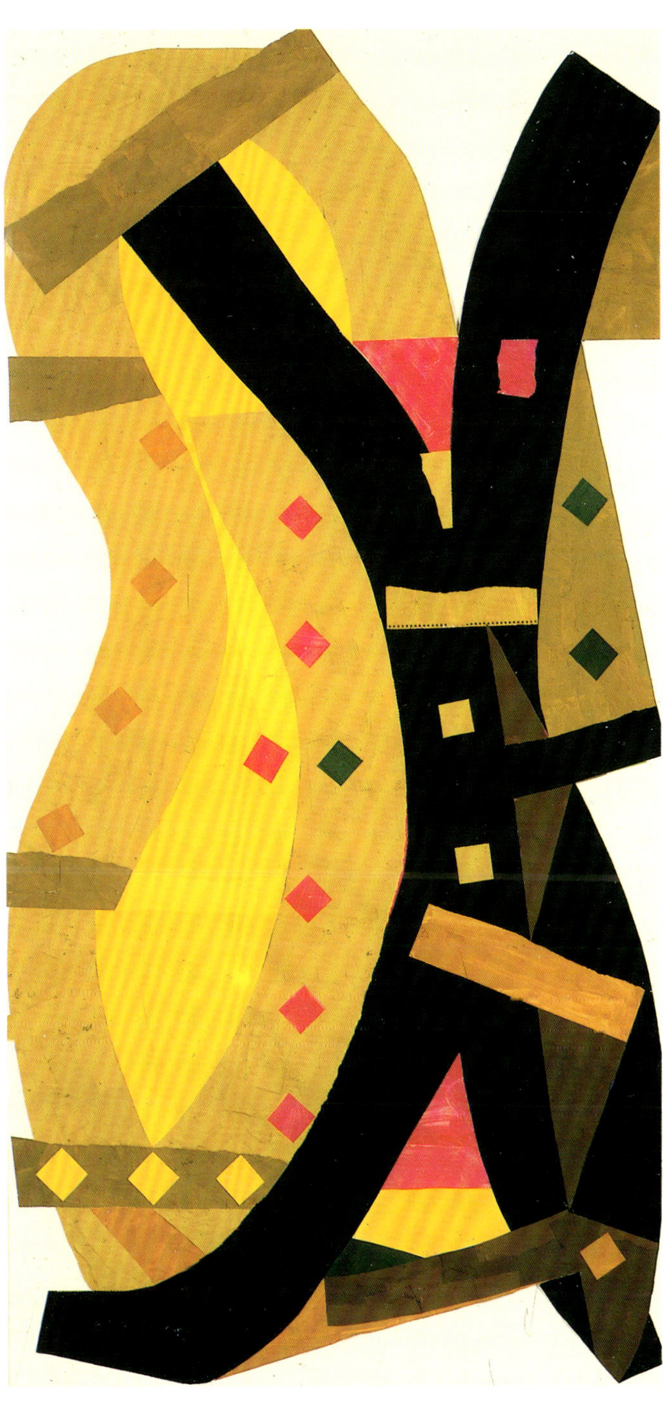

41

MARDI GRAS

1978

collage of painted papers

96 × 48

Lent by Hunter College of the City University of New York

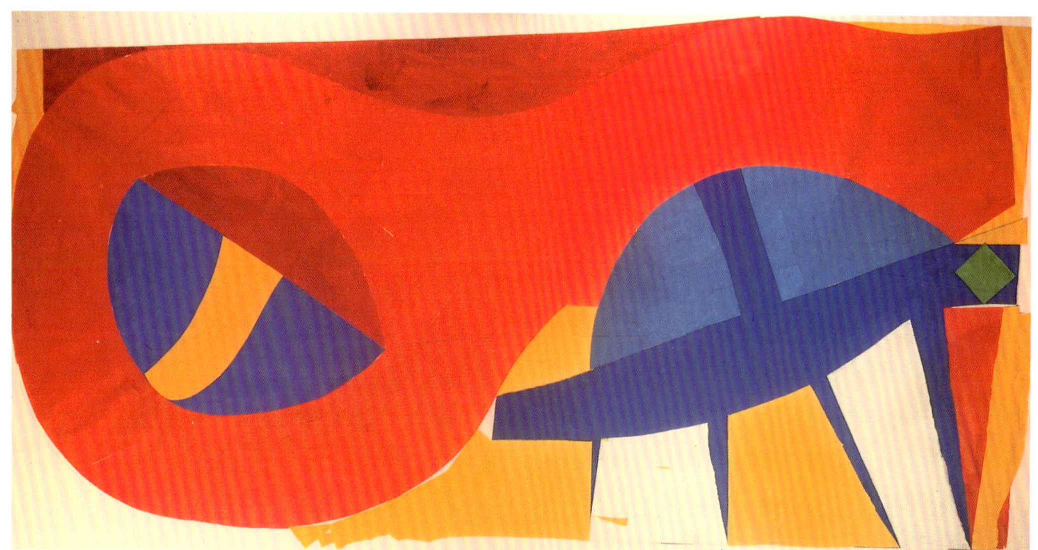

45

THE RED WAVE

1979

collage of painted papers

48 × 92

Lent by Ronnie and John Shore, Cincinnati, Ohio

46

1979

collage of painted papers

48 × 80

Lent by William Frankel, Wynnewood, Pennsylvania

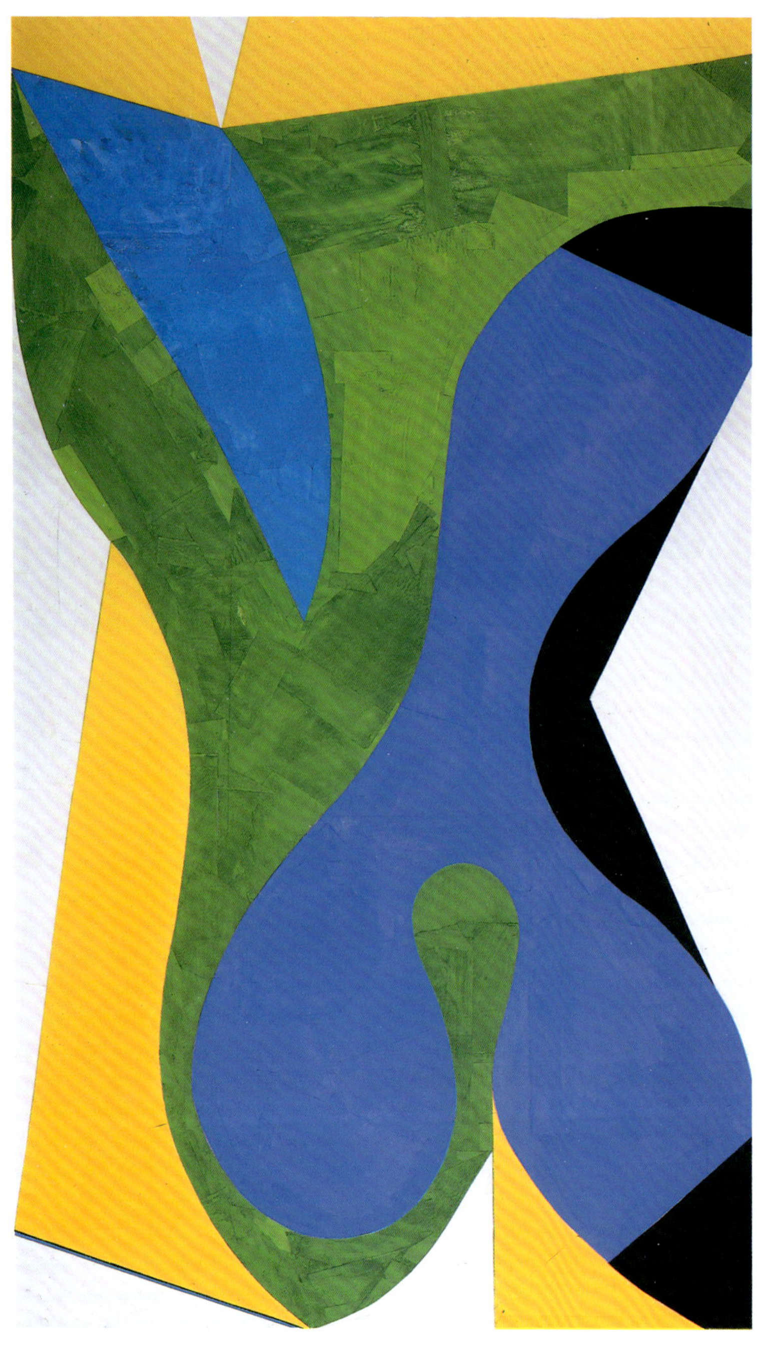

48

1980

collage of painted papers

76 x 44

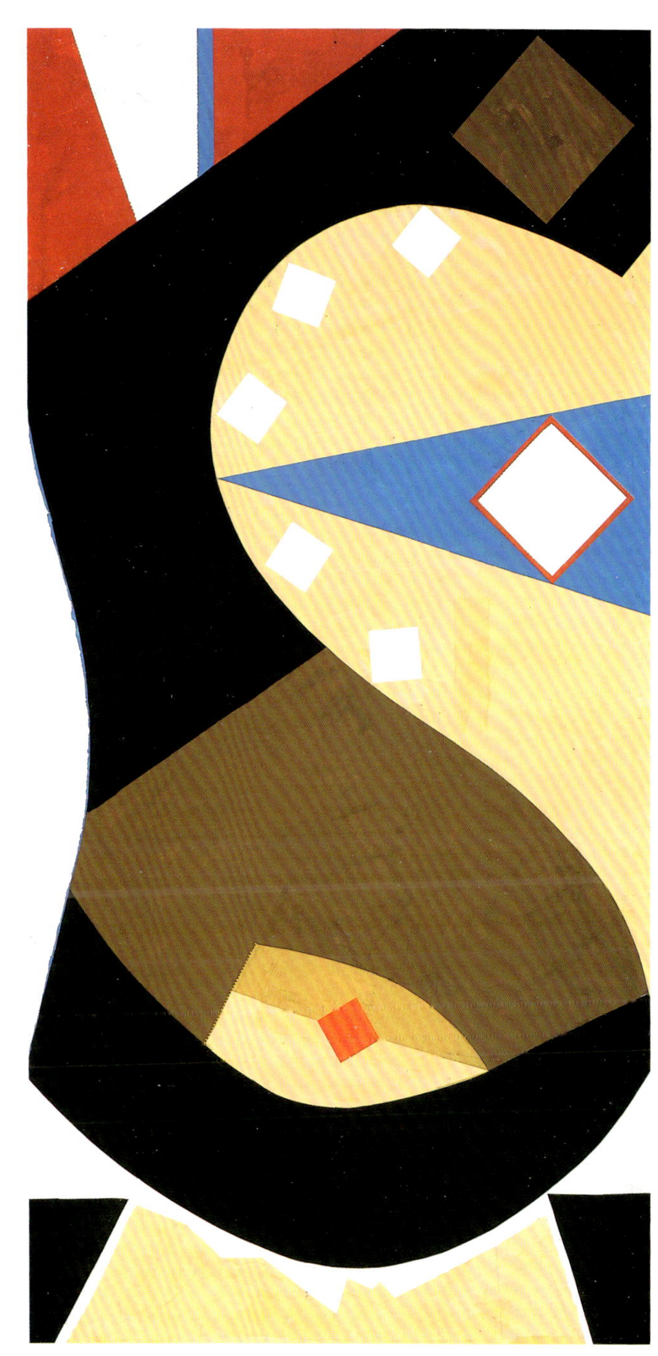

53

S E A W R A C K
1982
collage of painted papers
78 × 38

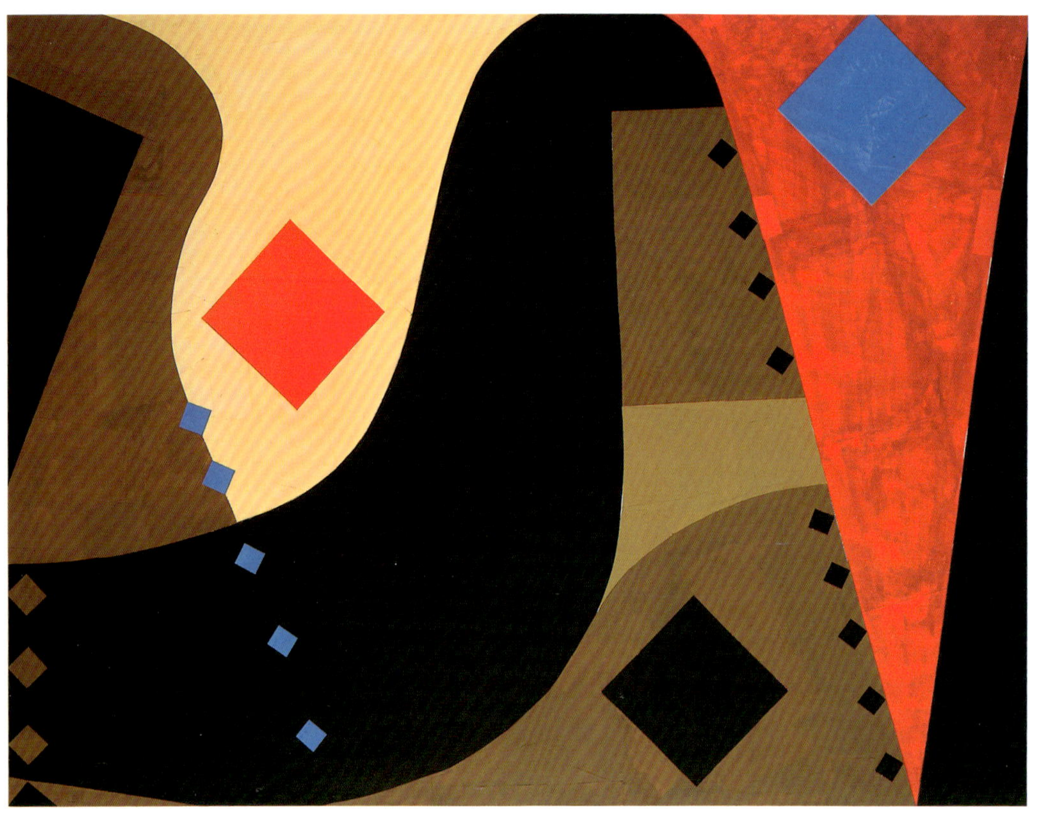

ANTE LUCE
1983
collage of painted papers
47 x 69

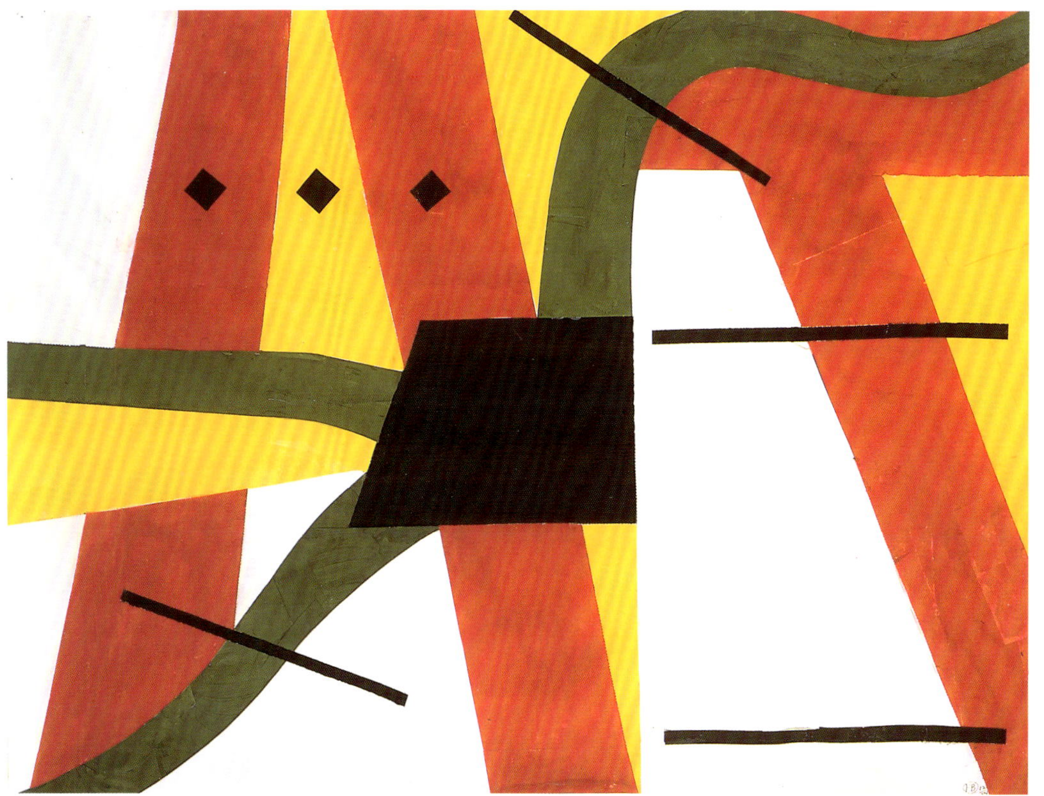

56

SPIDER

1985

collage of painted papers

30 × 40

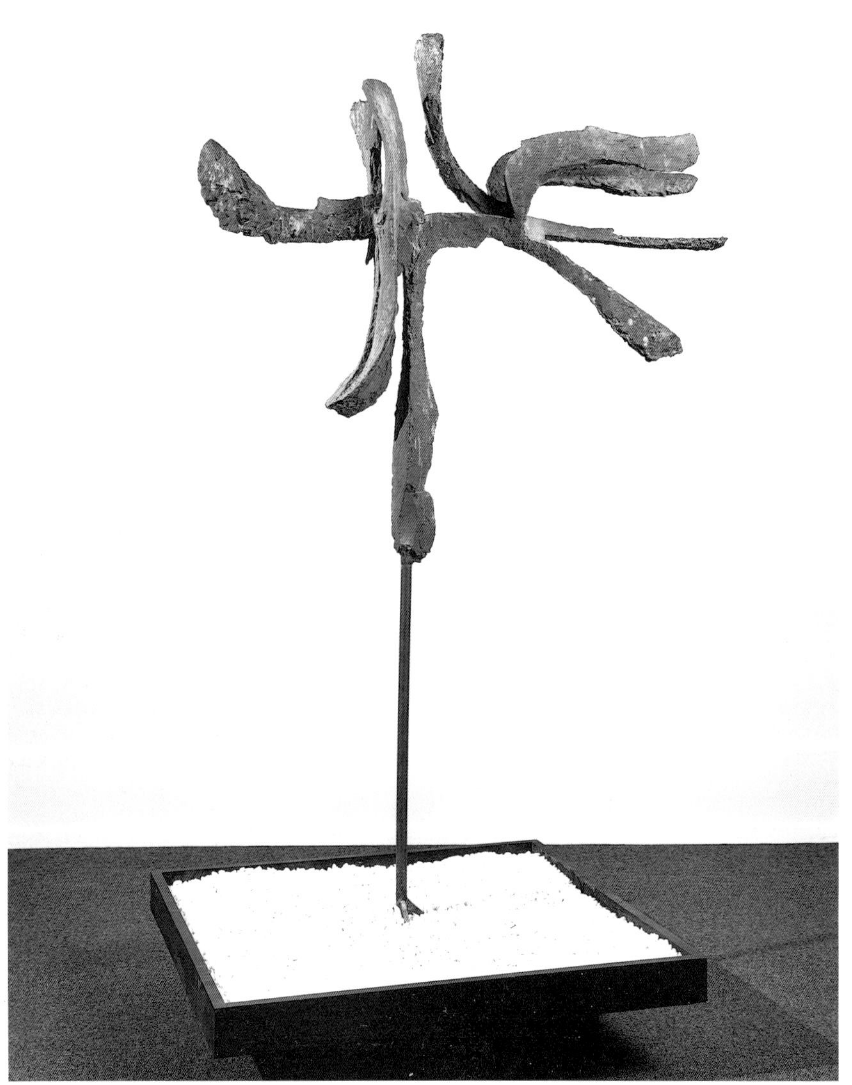

57

AZORES

1958

bronze

70 × 42 × 10

Lent by Bethany and Johann Bultman, New Orleans, Louisiana

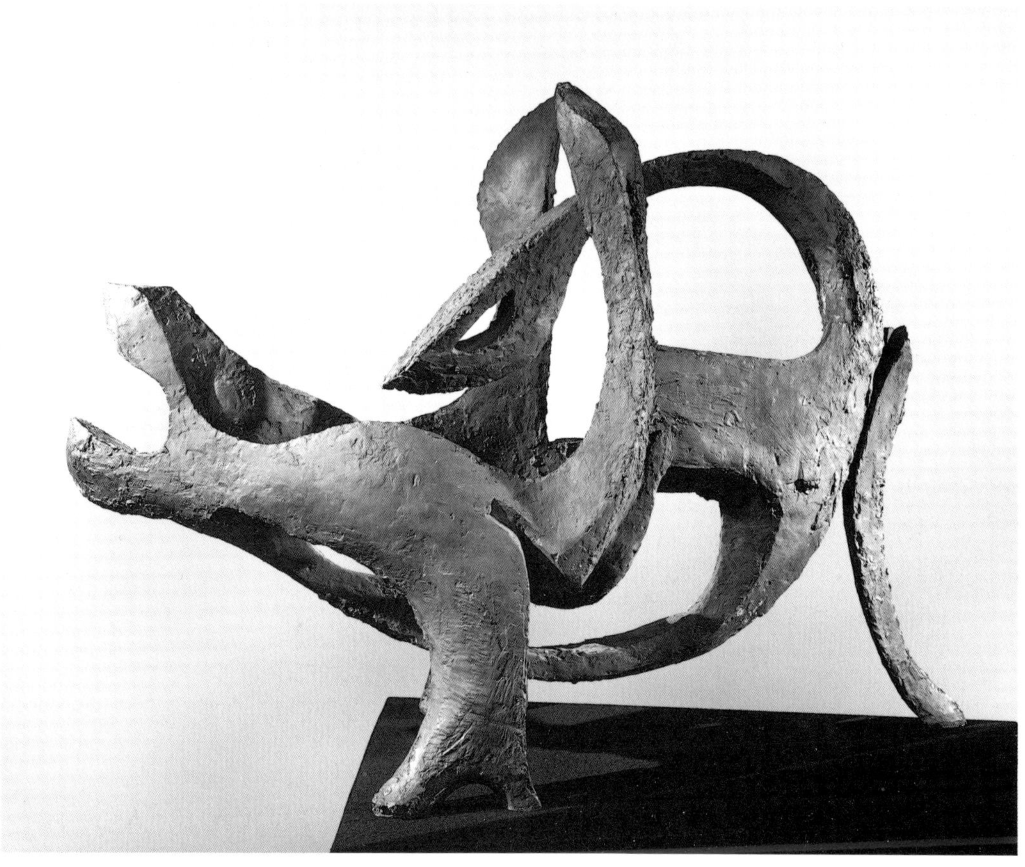

58

THE CRADLE

1958

bronze

29 × 42 × 20

Lent by Anthony F. Bultman, IV, New Orleans, Louisiana

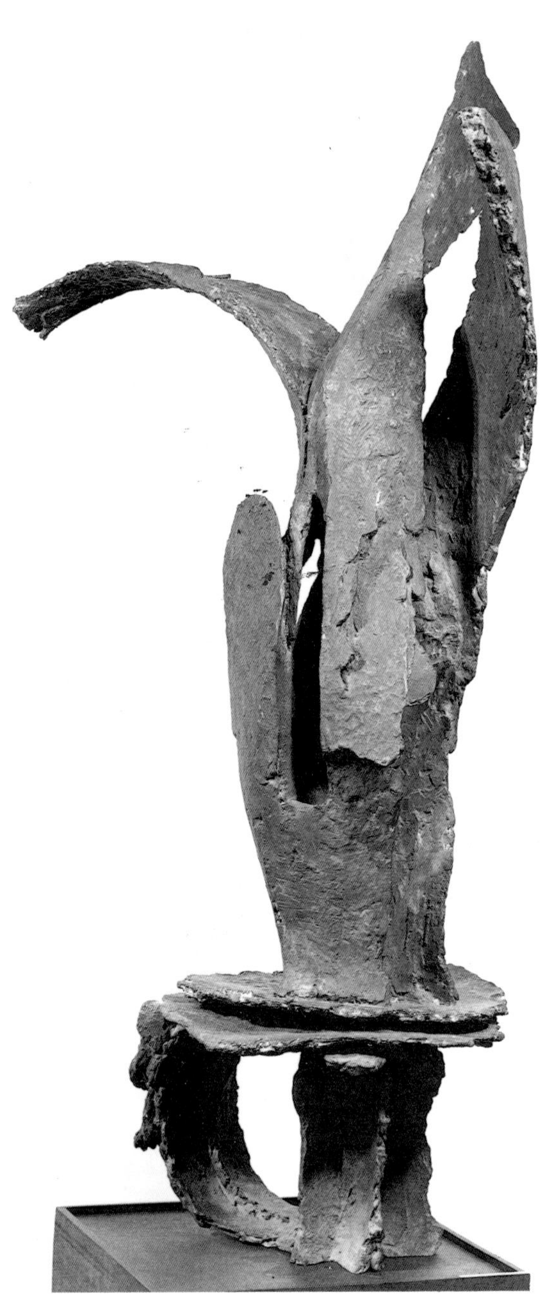

60

1961-62

b r o n z e

60 x 36 x 27

Lent by Whitney Museum of American Art, New York, New York

Purchase with funds from the Hans and Miz Hofmann Foundation, Inc.

COAT OF MALE
1962
unique bronze
20 × 20 × 4
Lent by Robert W. Ossorio, New York, New York

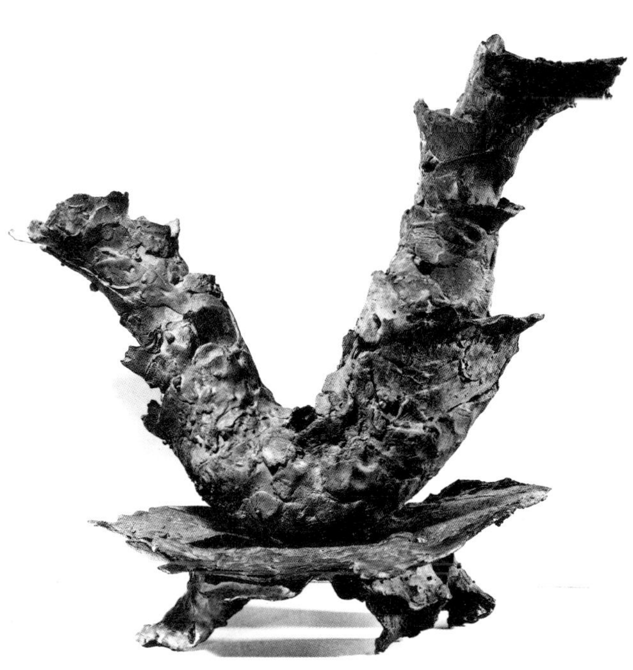

62

SEA SEASON
1962
unique bronze
13 × 14 × 9 1/2
Lent by Bethany and Johann Bultman, New Orleans, Louisiana

64

FIRE FOUNTAIN
1965
unique bronze
17 × 13¹/₂ × 7
Lent by William Frankel,
Wynnewood, Pennsylvania

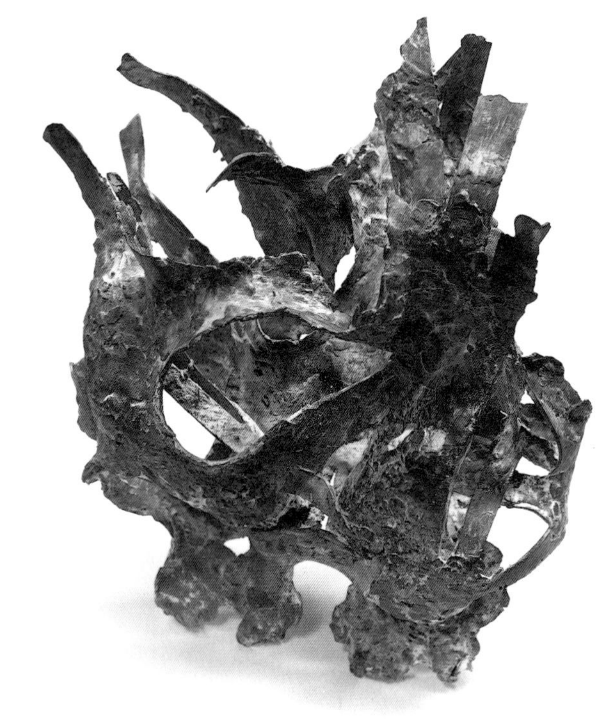

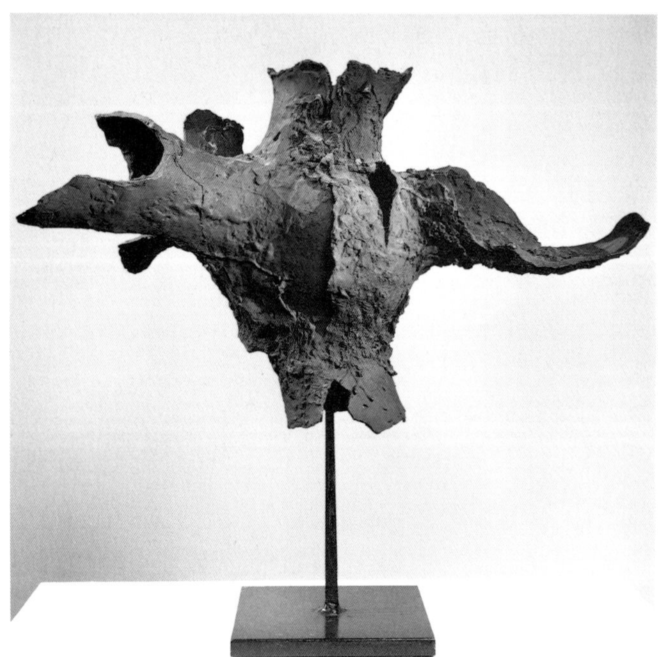

65

CRATER I
1965
unique bronze
17 × 19 × 8

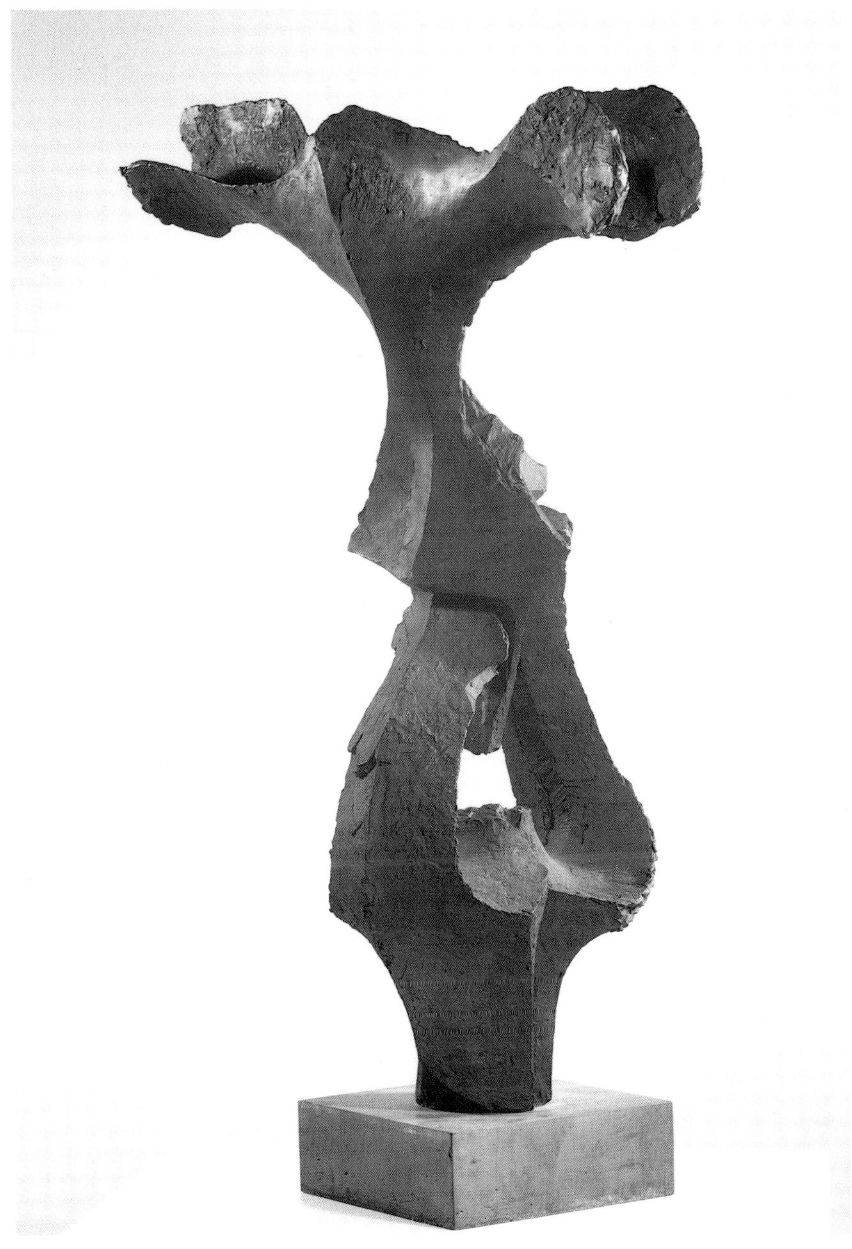

66

P O R T A G E

1972

b r o n z e

36 x 22 x 13

Lent by The Roger Houston Ogden Collection, New Orleans, Louisiana

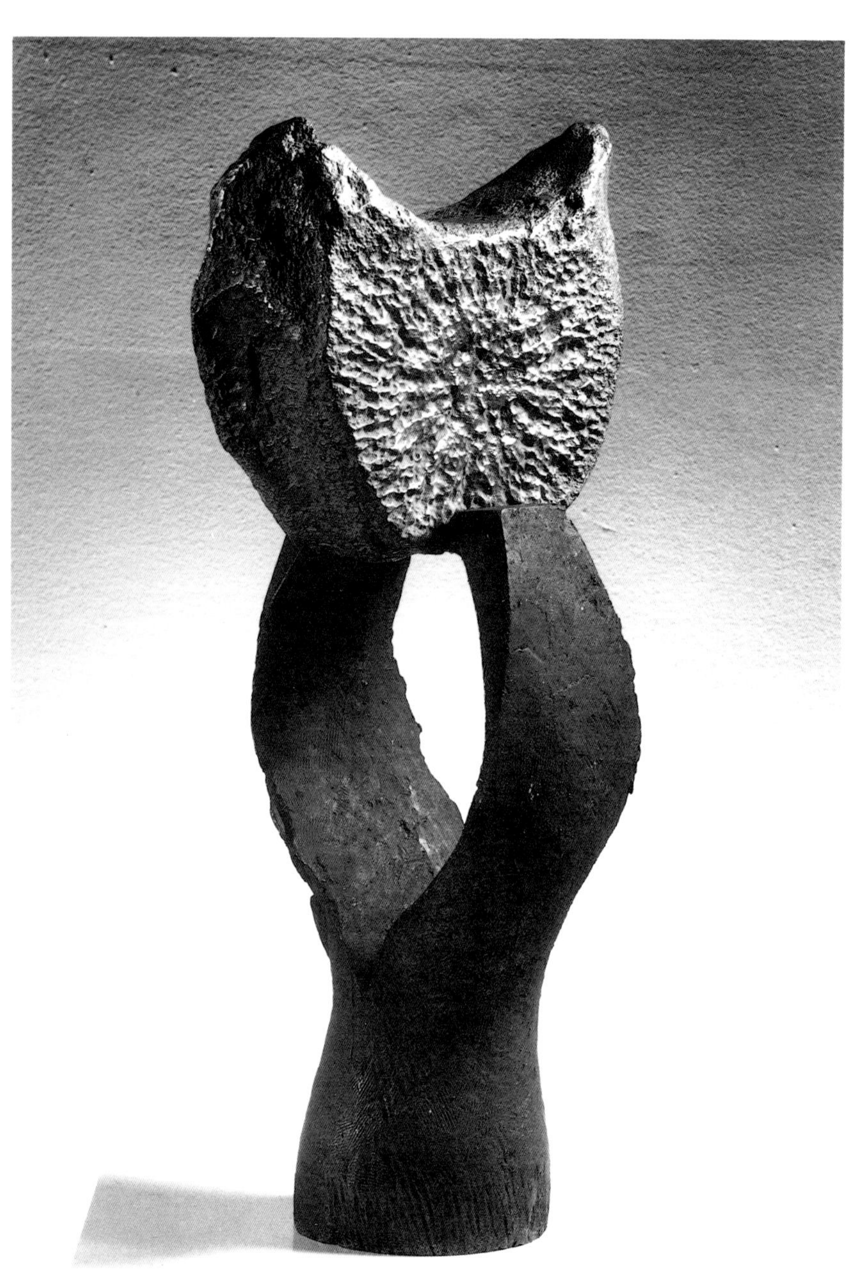

68

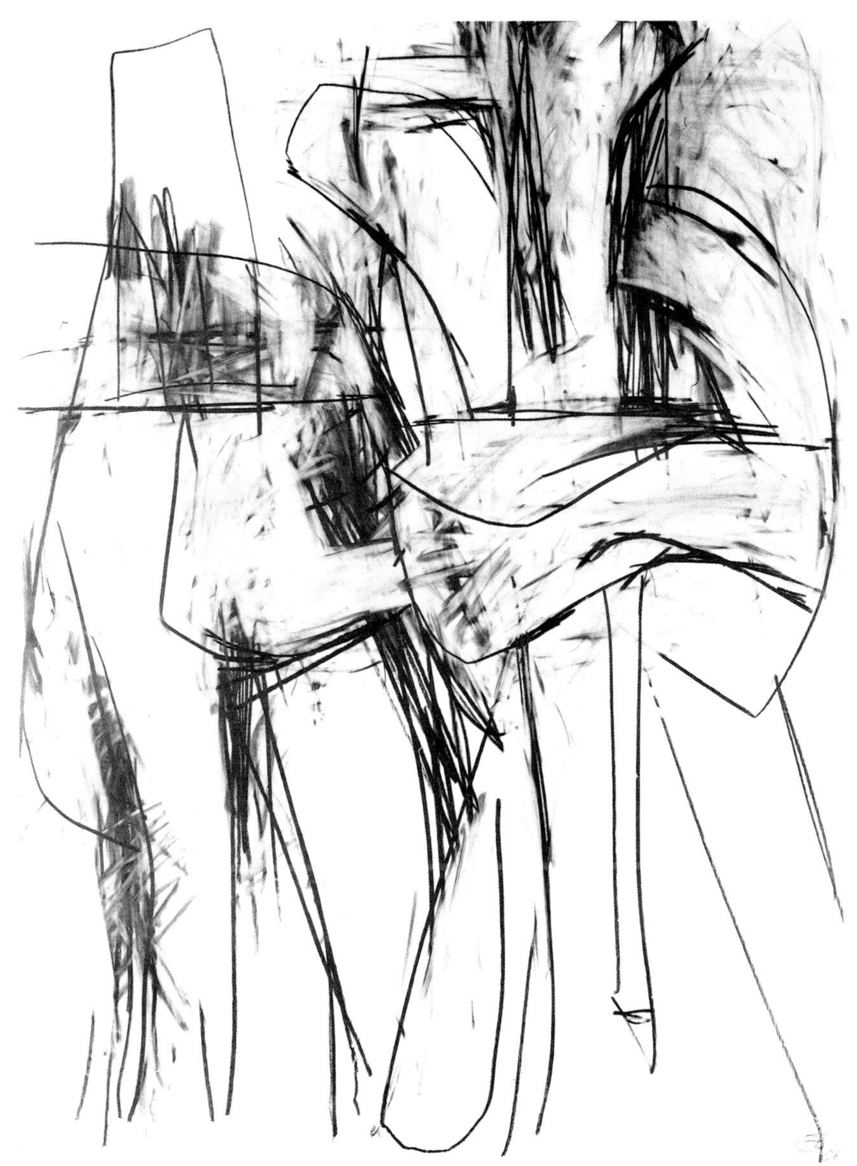

73

CLARETTA II
1958
pencil on paper
30 × 22

74

DON ON ONE LEG
1961
pencil on paper
29 × 23
Lent by The William Benton Museum of Art, Storrs, Connecticut

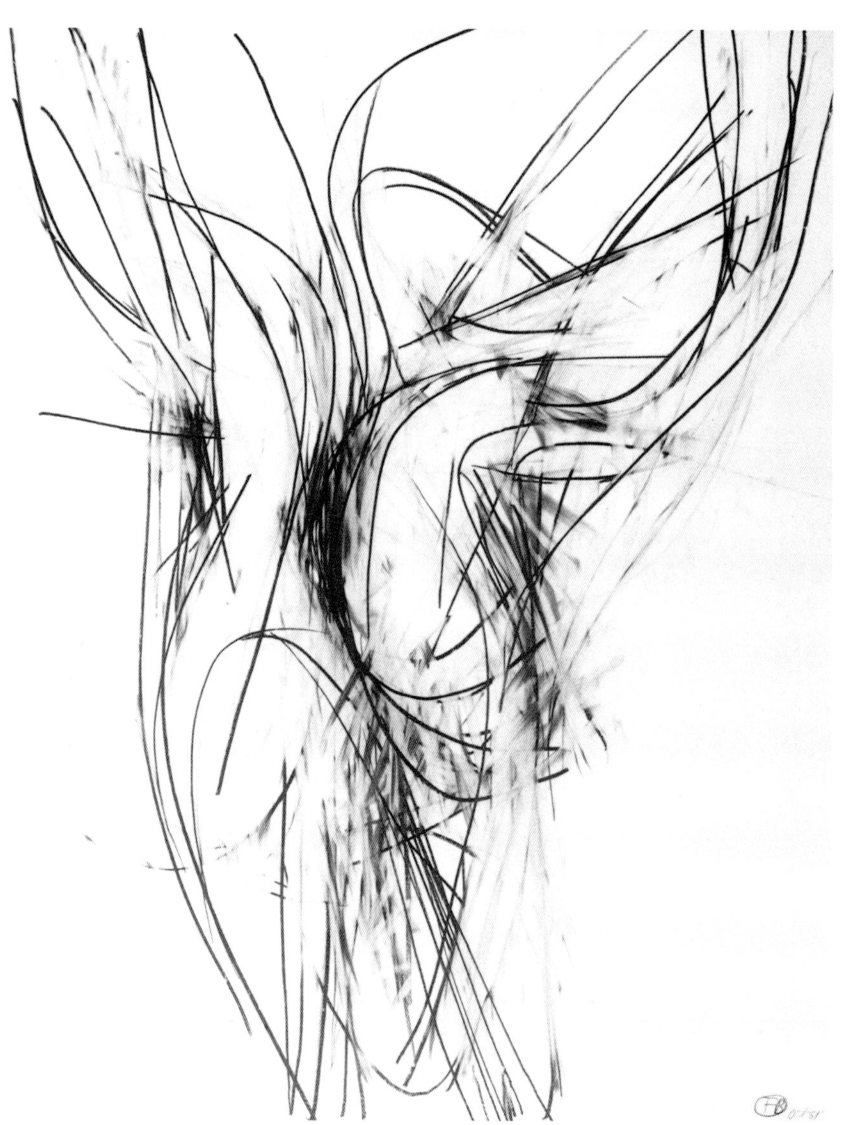

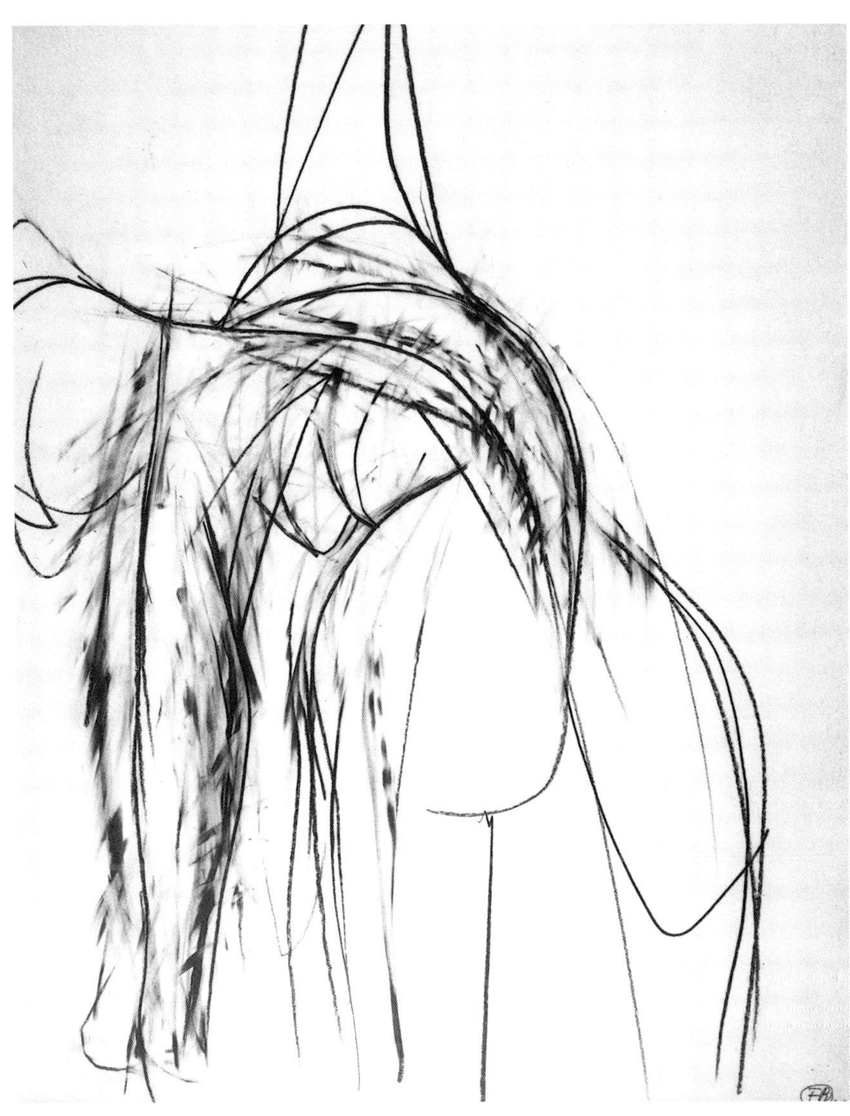

75

I V Y   I I
1961
pencil on paper
29 × 23

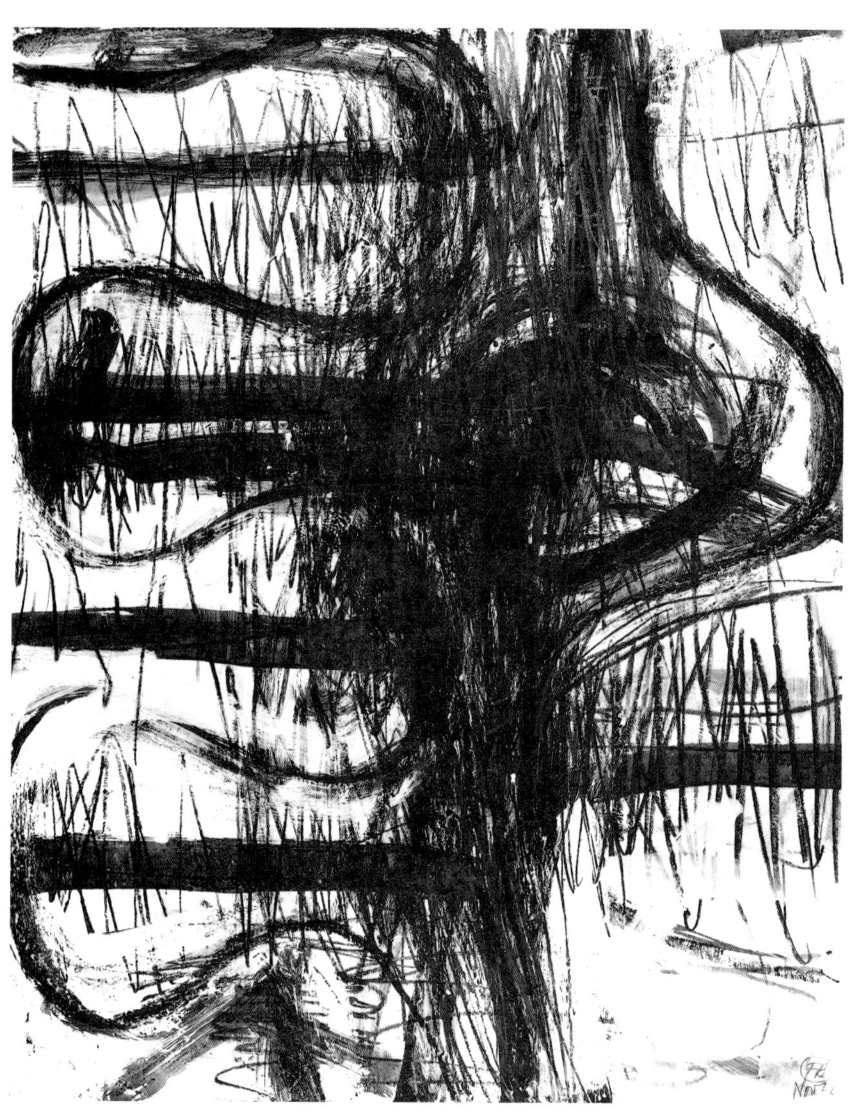

76

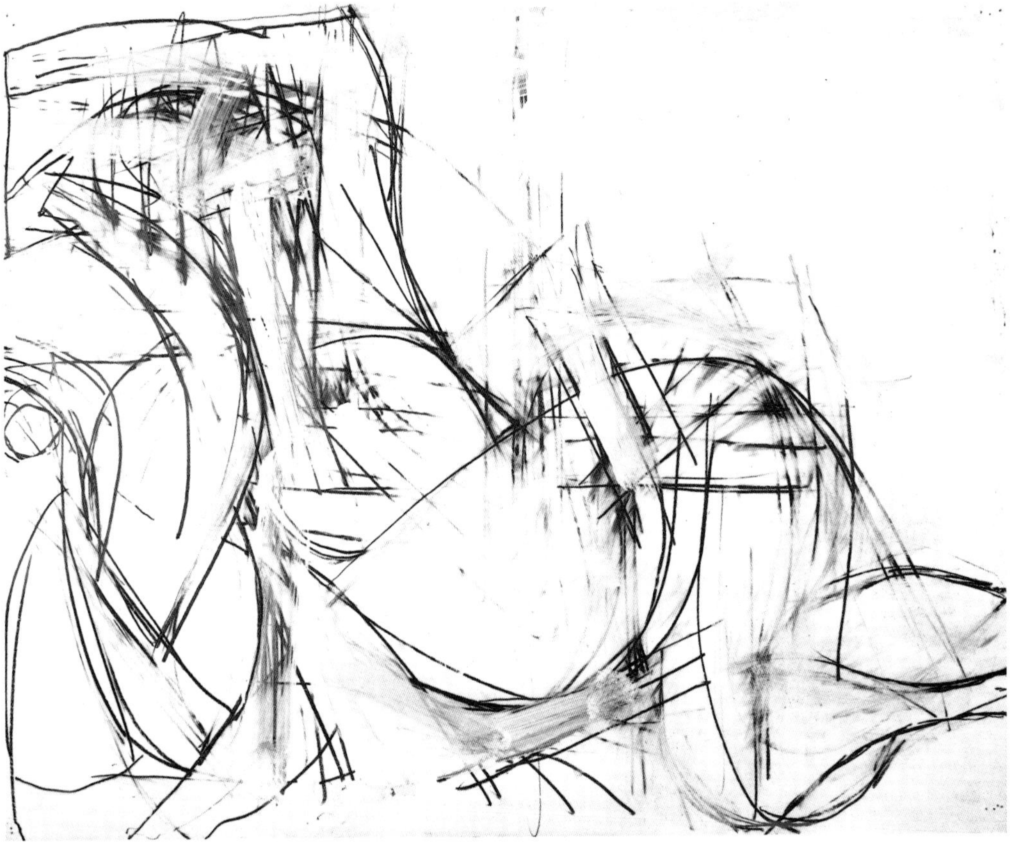

77

MIKI (ORIENTAL II)

1964

pencil on paper

23 × 29

Lent by National Museum of American Art, Smithsonian Institution, Washington, D.C.

Gift of Mr. and Mrs. David K. Anderson, Martha Jackson Memorial Collection

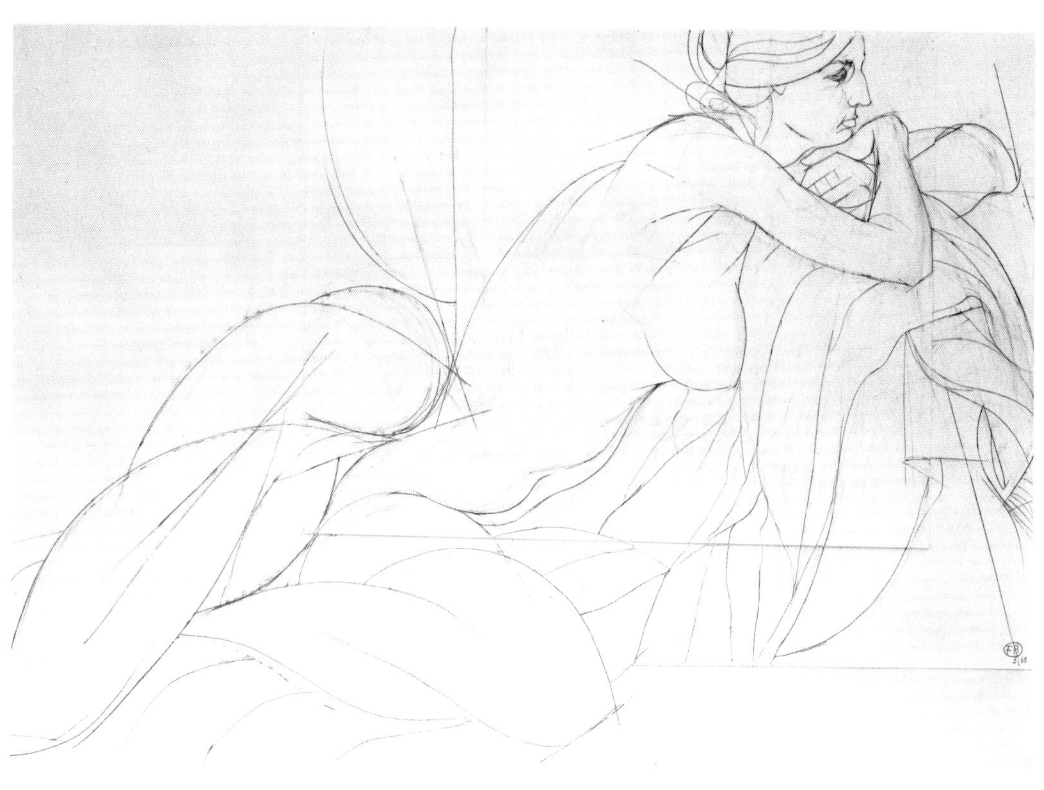

80

TACKE – CENTAUR
1968
pencil on paper
36 × 50

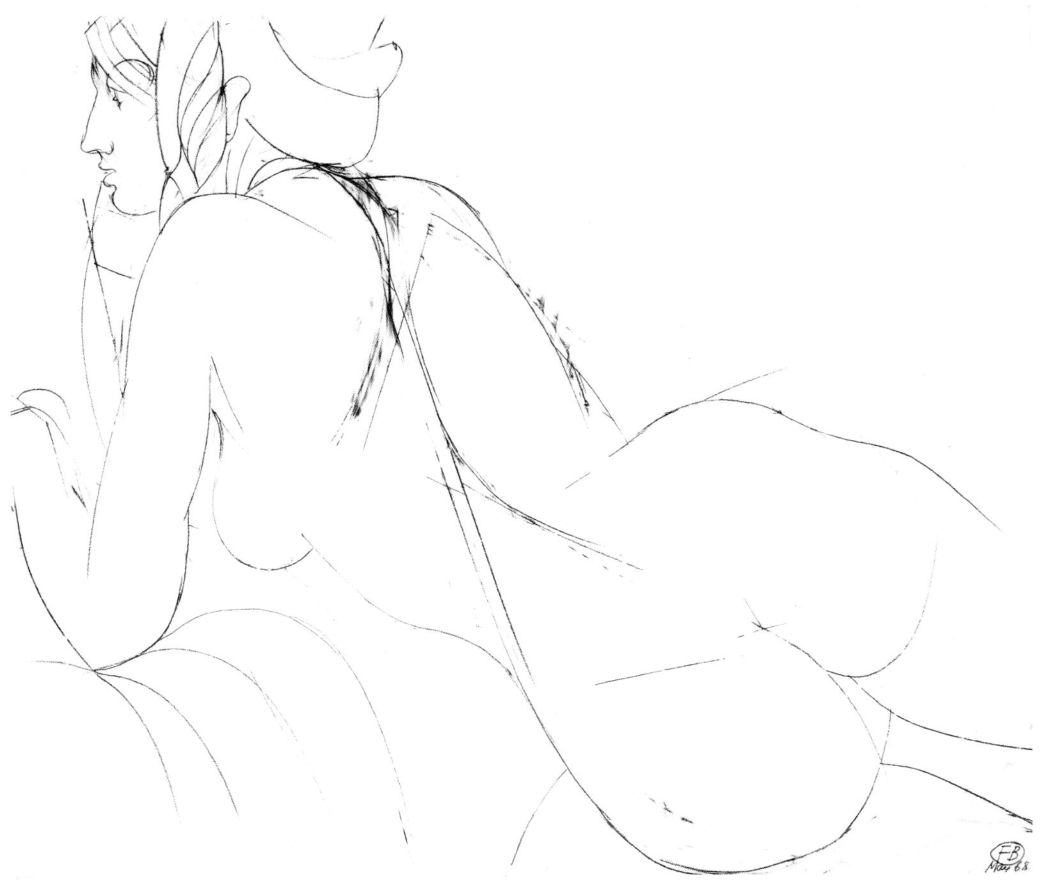

81

T A C K E – B R A I D E D H A I R

1968

pencil on paper

23 × 29

Lent by Mr. and Mrs. James S. Deely, New York, New York

83

T A C K E   –   S E A T E D
1970
p e n c i l   o n   p a p e r
29 × 23

Lent by Pat Sloane, Brooklyn, New York

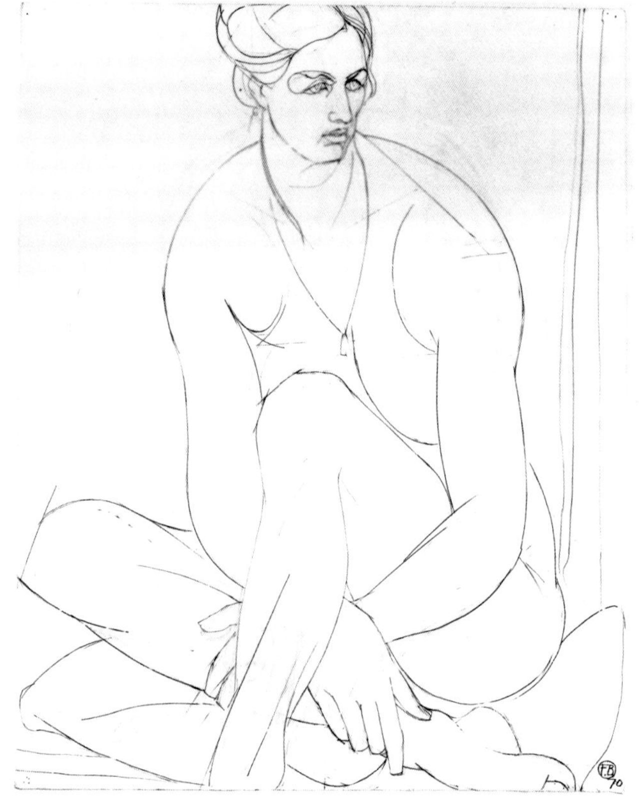

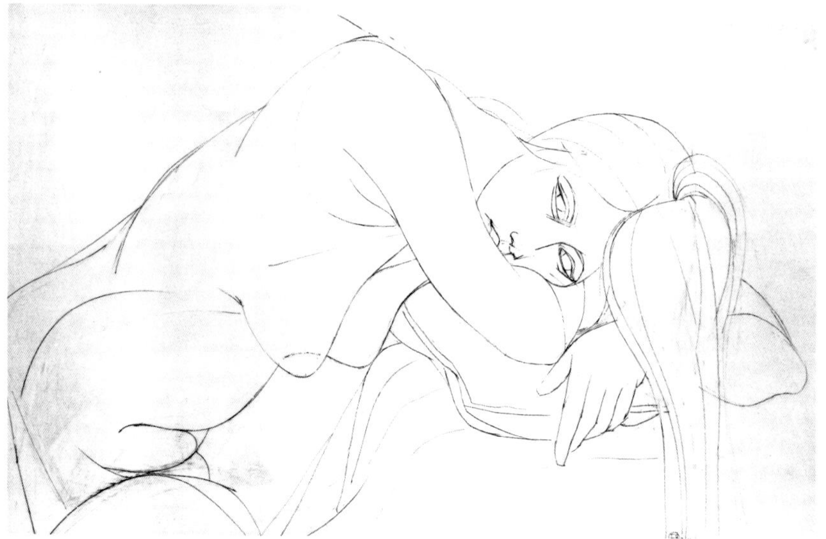

84

V I C K I   –   B R I D G E   I
1972
p e n c i l   o n   p a p e r
30 × 47¹/₂

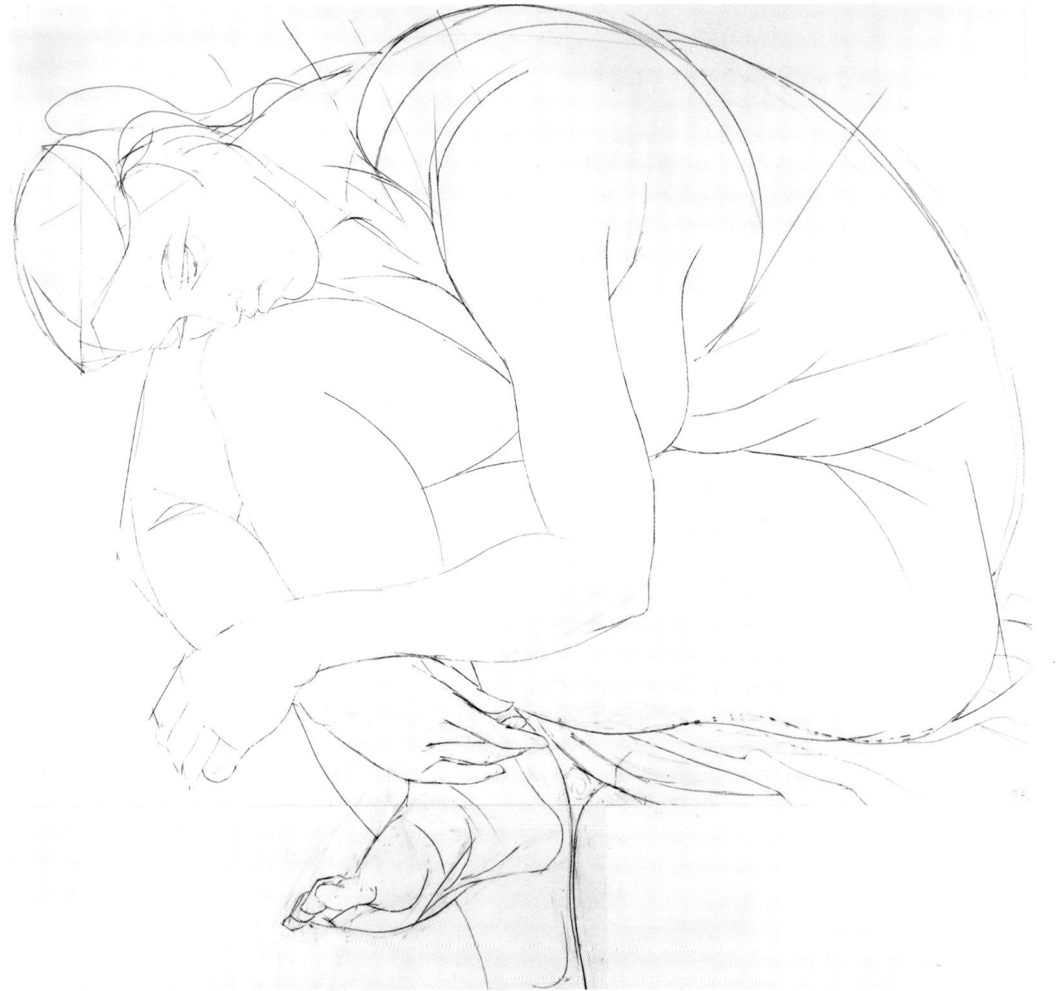

85

L A U R E L – S P I R A L

1973

p e n c i l   o n   p a p e r

38 × 44

Lent by Whitney Museum of American Art, New York, New York

Purchase with funds from an anonymous doner

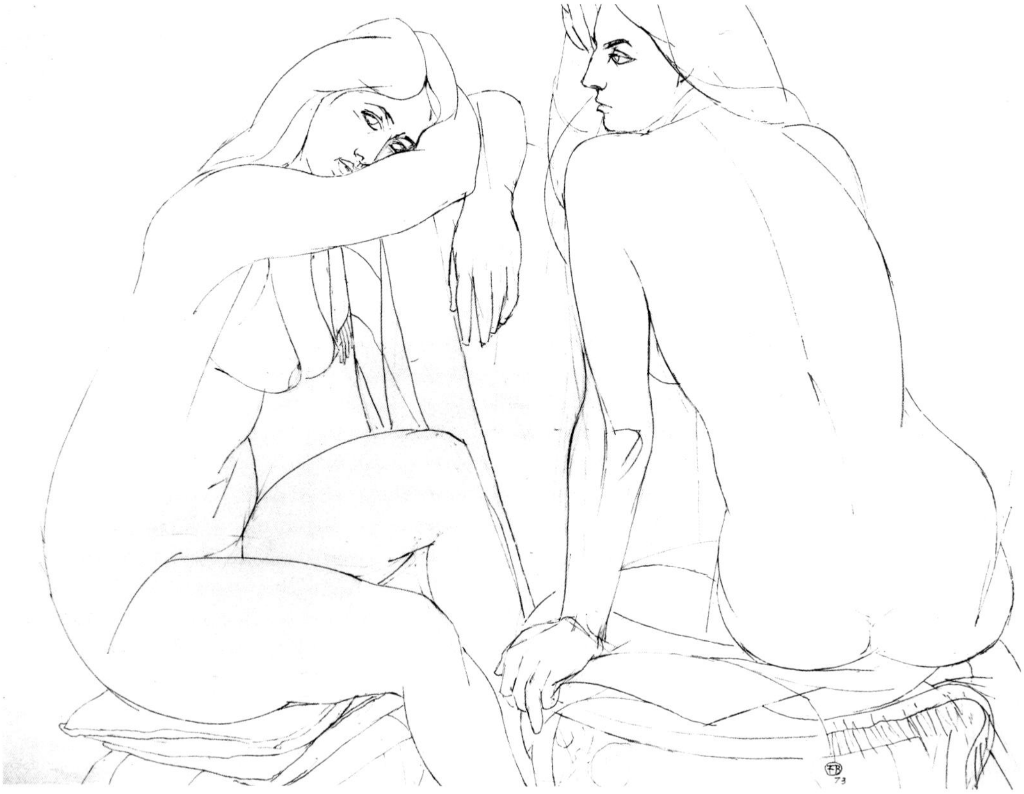

86

VICKI AND TACKE

1973

pencil on paper

30 × 40

New Orleans Museum of Art, The Muriel Bultman Francis Collection

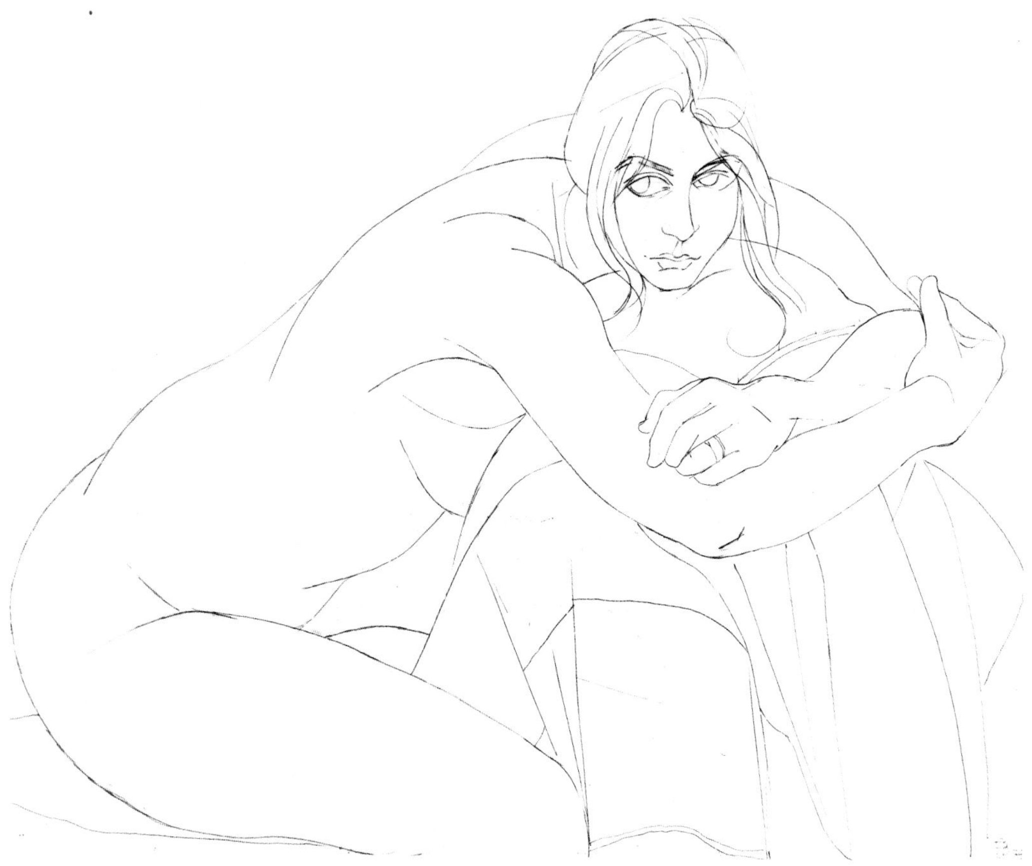

87

LORI — RECLINING

1974

pencil on paper

23 x 29

Lent by Ciba-Geigy Corporation, Ardsley, New York

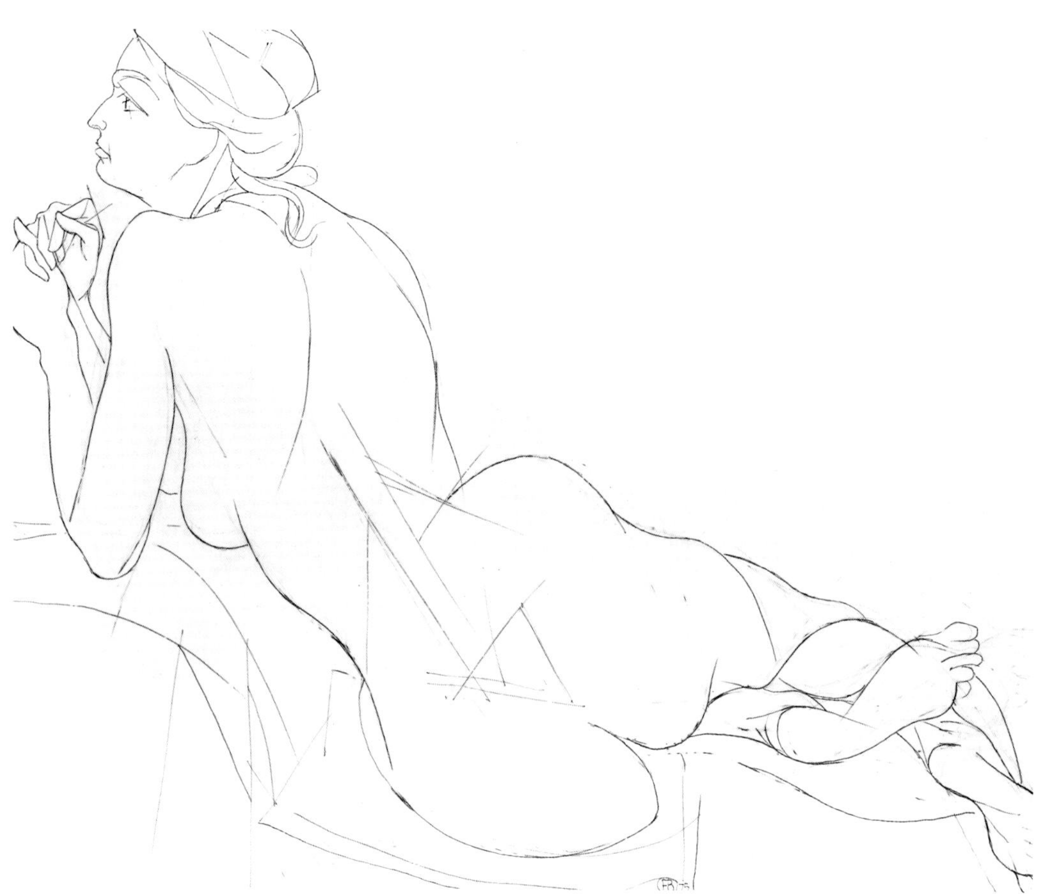

90

T A C K E – P R O W

1976

pencil on paper

23 × 29

Lent by Vera and Stephen L. Schlesinger, New York, New York

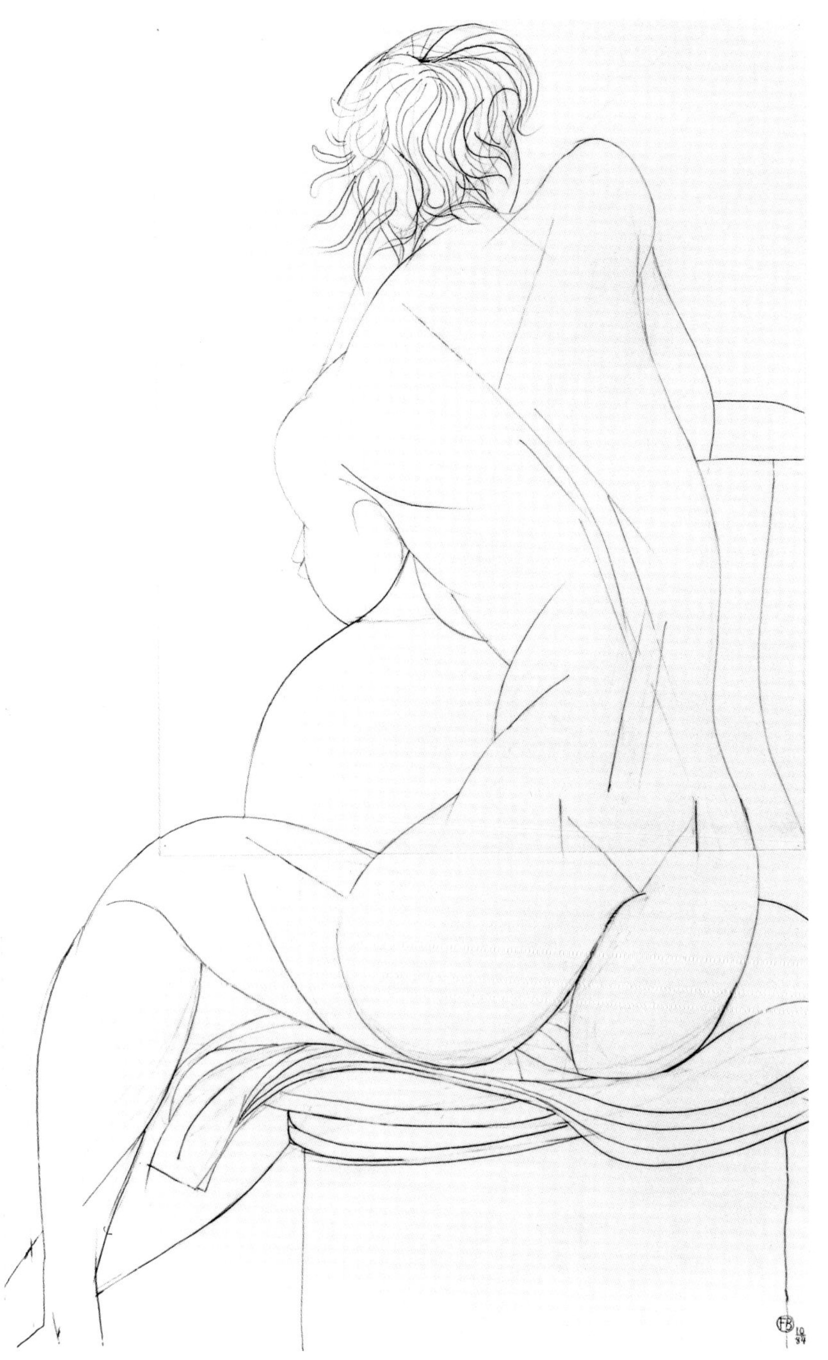

93

NICOLE'S BACK
1984
pencil on paper
47 x 29

All measurements are in inches, height preceding width, preceding depth. Illustrated works are indicated by an asterisk ★. Works traveling to other venues after the New Orleans showing are indicated by a dagger †. All works listed without a specific lender's name are lent by the estate of the artist and are courtesy of Gallery Schlesinger Limited in New York and Tilden-Foley Gallery in New Orleans.

PAINTINGS

1 ★
ACTEON MASK
STILL LIFE
1941
oil on canvas
30 × 24
Lent by The Roger Houston Ogden Collection, New Orleans, Louisiana

2 †
ACTEON
1945
oil on canvas
40 × 34

3
DOORKEEPER
1947
oil on canvas
31 × 46
New Orleans Museum of Art, The Muriel Bultman Francis Collection

4 †
SPECTATOR – RED AND BLACK
1947
tempera on board
40 × 32
Lent by Vincent Durham-Smith, Embreville, Pennsylvania

5 ★ †
THE WHITE READER
1949
oil on canvas
40 × 36

6 ★
THE HUNTER
1949
oil on celotex
60 × 48

7 †
THE BLACK KING
1949
oil on canvas
60 × 28

8 ★ †
THE RED KING
1949
oil on celotex
64 × 28

9
SPECTATOR I
1950
oil on canvas
36 × 42
Lent by Anthony F. Bultman, IV, New Orleans, Louisiana

10 ★ †
VIA PORTA ROMANA
1952
oil on masonite
96 × 36

11
SLEEPER, NUMBER 2
1952
oil on canvas
30 × 38
Lent by Whitney Museum of American Art, New York, New York Purchase

12 ★ †
INTERIOR – RAIN
1953
oil on canvas
38 × 49 1/2

13 ★ †
FROM THE DOOR
1954
oil on panel
14 × 10

14
SUN FIGURE
1955
oil on canvas
72 × 36
New Orleans Museum of Art, The Muriel Bultman Francis Collection

15 ★ †
SKIN OF THE NEGRESS
1957
oil on canvas
48 × 48

16 ★
ROSA PARK
1958
oil on canvas
72 × 108

17 †
THE SWEAT OF NIGHT
1958
oil on panel
20 × 24

18
THE DELTA
1959
oil on canvas
72 × 48
Lent by National Museum of American Art, Smithsonian Institution, Washington, D.C., Gift of Mr. and Mrs. David K. Anderson, Martha Jackson Memorial Collection

19 ★ †
COOL GATE
1960
oil on canvas
96 × 48

20
GRAVITY OF NIGHTFALL
1961
oil on canvas-triptych panels
96 × 144

21 ★
THIRD
1961
oil on canvas
48 × 96

22 ★
M OVER W
1961
oil on canvas
96 × 72

23
GREEK
1962
oil on canvas
72 × 48
Lent by Arthur M. Huntington Art
Gallery, University of Texas at Austin
Gift of the Artist

24 ★ †
JULY
1962
oil on canvas
96 × 72

25
TISHAMINGO
1962
oil on canvas
72 × 48
Lent by Weatherspoon Art Gallery,
University of North Carolina
at Greensboro
Gift of Mr. A. Fred Bultman

26
DEPART – GOOD NEWS
(4 panels)
1965
oil on canvas
76 1/2 × 115

27
THE NURSE, THE
CHAUFFEUR
(2 curved panels)
1968
oil on canvas
96 × 48

28
NIGHT BIRD
1974
oil on canvas
80 × 100

29 ★
INTRUSION OF BLUE
1974
oil on canvas
72 × 96

30 ★ †
THE BLUE WAVE
1983
oil on canvas
48 × 58

COLLAGES

31 ★ †
OLD GOLD
1938
collage of painted papers
19 1/2 × 22 3/4

32 †
LOVERS
1962
collage of painted papers
29 × 23
Lent by Vera and Stephen L.
Schlesinger, New York, New York

33 ★ †
ILIUM
1966
collage of painted papers
23 × 29
Lent by Mrs. George P. Kramer,
New York, New York

34 †
WAVE OVER LAP
1967
collage of painted papers
48 × 38

35
UNTWINING
1968
collage with gouache and
graphite
29 × 23
Lent by the Estate of Judith
Rothschild, New York, New York

36
MAKING THE ELEMENT
1973
collage of painted papers
51 × 77
Lent by Tulane University, New
Orleans, Louisiana

37 †
SKYHOOK
1973
collage of painted papers
74 × 48
Lent by Joan and Michael Nelson

38 ★ †
WINTERSIGNS
1975
collage of painted papers
48 × 78

39
THE WAY UP AND THE
WAY DOWN
1975
collage of painted papers
90 1/2 × 48
Lent by National Museum of
American Art, Smithsonian
Institution, Washington, D.C.,
Gift of Mr. and Mrs. David K.
Anderson, Martha Jackson
Memorial Collection

40 ★ †
THE BEACH
1978
collage of painted papers
86 × 48

41 ★ †
MARDI GRAS
1978
collage of painted papers
96 × 48
Lent by Hunter College of the City
University of New York

42
NOVEMBER WAVE
1978
collage of painted papers
53 × 53
Lent by the Montclair Art Museum,
Montclair, New Jersey, Museum
Purchase: Mr. and Mrs. S. Barksdale
Perrick, Jr. Fund

43 ★
THE RED WAVE
1979
collage of painted papers
48 × 92
Lent by Ronnie and John Shore,
Cincinnati, Ohio

44 †
CONSTELLATION
1979
collage of painted papers
and push pins
31 × 34

45 †
CAPE MAY II
1979
collage of painted papers
24 × 30
Lent by Ruth S. Latta, Provincetown,
Massachusetts

46 ★
THE BLUE WAVE I
1979
collage of painted papers
48 × 80
Lent by William Frankel,
Wynnewood, Pennsylvania

47
UPWELLING
1979
collage of painted papers
and push pins
48 × 88

48 ★
FLOATING II
1980
collage of painted papers
76 × 44

49 †
OTHER
1981
collage of painted papers
52 × 46

50 †
AURAT
1982
collage of painted papers
48 × 76

51 †
GARDEN SPRING
1982
collage of painted papers
96 × 48

52
BLUE WAVE II
1982
collage of painted papers
48 × 80
Lent by Anka and Louis Begley,
New York, New York

53 ★ †
SEAWRACK
1982
collage of painted papers
78 × 38

54 ★ †
ANTE LUCE
1983
collage of painted papers
47 × 69

55
NOTTE
1983
collage of painted papers
48 × 37 1/2

56 ★ †
SPIDER
1985
collage of painted papers
30 × 40

SCULPTURE

57 ★
AZORES
1958
bronze
70 × 42 × 10
Lent by Bethany and Johann
Bultman, New Orleans, Louisiana

58 ★
THE CRADLE
1958
bronze
29 × 42 × 20
Lent by Anthony F. Bultman, IV,
New Orleans, Louisiana

59
THE GATE
1960
bronze
72 × 42 × 25
Lent by William Frankel,
Wynnewood, Pennsylvania

60 ★
VASE OF THE WINDS II
1961-62
bronze
60 × 36 × 27
Lent by Whitney Museum of
American Art, New York, New York
Purchase with funds from the Hans
and Miz Hofmann Foundation, Inc.

61 ★
COAT OF MALE
1962
unique bronze
20 × 20 × 4
Lent by Robert W. Ossorio,
New York, New York

62 ★
SEA SEASON
1962
unique bronze
13 × 14 × 9 1/2
Lent by Bethany and Johann
Bultman, New Orleans, Louisiana

63 †
THE PART
1964
unique bronze
8 × 14 × 7 1/2

64 ★
FIRE FOUNTAIN
1965
unique bronze
17 × 13 1/2 × 7
Lent by William Frankel,
Wynnewood, Pennsylvania

65 ★ †
CRATER I
1965
unique bronze
17 × 19 × 8

66 ★
PORTAGE
1972
bronze
36 × 22 × 13
Lent by The Roger Houston Ogden
Collection, New Orleans, Louisiana

67
BARRIER III
1972
unique bronze
13 × 24 × 6
Lent by Solomon R. Guggenheim
Museum, New York, New York

68 ★ †
WISHBONE
1972
bronze
19 × 10 × 7

69 †
HOPE!
1973
bronze
70 × 55 × 22

70 †
HEAD: OWL'S EYE
1973
unique bronze
20 1/2 × 13 1/2 × 9
Lent by Abby and B. H. Friedman,
New York, New York

71 †
GARDEN AT
NIGHTFALL I
1977
unique bronze
17 × 9 × 9

72 †
WAVE
1977
bronze
22 × 38 × 16

DRAWINGS

73 ★ †
CLARETTA II
1958
pencil on paper
30 × 22

74 ★
DON ON ONE LEG
1961
pencil on paper
29 × 23
*Lent by The William Benton
Museum of Art, Storrs, Connecticut*

75 ★ †
IVY II
1961
pencil on paper
29 × 23

76 ★ †
UNO
1962
mixed media
29 × 23

77
MIKI (ORIENTAL II)
1964
pencil on paper
23 × 29
*Lent by National Museum of
American Art, Smithsonian
Institution, Washington, D.C.
Gift of Mr. and Mrs. David K.
Anderson, Martha Jackson
Memorial Collection*

78 ★ †
MIKI
1964
pencil on paper
23 × 29

79 †
RAMON STANDING
1965
pencil on paper
25 1/2 × 22

80 ★ †
TACKE – CENTAUR
1968
pencil on paper
36 × 50

81 ★
TACKE – BRAIDED
HAIR
1968
pencil on paper
23 × 29
*Lent by Mr. and Mrs. James S.
Deely, New York, New York*

82 †
LYNN AND TACKE
1968
pencil on paper
23 × 29

83 ★
TACKE – SEATED
1970
pencil on paper
29 × 23
*Lent by Pat Sloane,
Brooklyn, New York*

84 ★ †
VICKI – BRIDGE I
1972
pencil on paper
30 × 47 1/2

85 ★
LAUREL – SPIRAL
1973
pencil on paper
38 × 44
*Lent by Whitney Museum of
American Art, New York, New York
Purchase with funds from an
anonymous doner*

86 ★
VICKI AND TACKE
1973
pencil on paper
30 × 40
*New Orleans Museum of Art, The
Muriel Bultman Francis Collection*

87 ★
LORI – RECLINING
1974
pencil on paper
23 × 29
*Lent by Ciba-Geigy Corporation,
Ardsley, New York*

88 †
TACKE – REPRISE
1975
pencil on paper
45 × 44

89
LORI – ARCH OF
SUMMER
1975
pencil on paper
23 × 45
*Lent by Jo Ann Hirshhorn, Metairie,
Louisiana*

90 ★
TACKE – PROW
1976
pencil on paper
23 × 29
*Lent by Vera and Stephen L.
Schlesinger, New York, New York*

91 †
LORI – ARC EN CIEL
1977
pencil on paper
30 × 40

92
FIONA
1981
pencil on paper
23 × 29
*Lent by Clarence Cukor, Wilton,
Connecticut*

93 ★ †
NICOLE'S BACK
1984
pencil on paper
47 × 29

94 †
GROUP OF SIX LAST
DRAWINGS
1985
pencil on paper
14 × 9

BIOGRAPHICAL CHRONOLOGY

1919   Born April 4, New Orleans, Louisiana

1931   Began to study art with Morris Graves, New Orleans, Louisiana

1932-35   Studied at Arts and Crafts Club, New Orleans, Louisiana

1935-37   Attended Munich Prepatory School, Germany; painted and traveled in Europe

1937-38   Attended the New Bauhaus, Chicago, Illinois

1938-41   Studied with Hans Hofmann, Provincetown, Massachusetts and New York, New York

1943   Married Jeanne Lawson

1950-51   Received Italian government grant for Exchange Fellowship, Florence, Italy; studied bronze casting

1952   First show at Kootz Gallery, New York, New York

1958   Instructor in design, Pratt Institute, New York, New York

1959   First show at Martha Jackson Gallery, New York, New York

1959-63   Graduate school instructor in painting, Hunter College, New York, New York

1962-63   Instructor in painting, Pratt Institute, New York, New York

1964   Received sculpture award, *American Show*, Art Institute of Chicago, Chicago, Illinois

1964-65   Received Fulbright Fellowship for study in Paris, France

1968-72   Instructor at Fine Arts Work Center, Provincetown, Massachusetts

1974   Guest lecturer at Department of Architecture, Tulane University, New Orleans, Louisiana

1975   Received Solomon R. Guggenheim Grant, New York, New York

1977   Lectured on Hans Hofmann at Hirshhorn Museum and Sculpture Garden, Washington, D.C.

1978   Traveled and studied in Turkey

1978   Lectured and taught at University of Western Carolina, Cullowhee, North Carolina

1978-79   Guest lecturer at Tulane University, New Orleans, Louisiana

1979   Lectured and taught at Tougaloo College, Tougaloo, Mississippi

1980   Guest lecturer at Parsons School of Design, New York, New York

1981   Artist-in-Residence, Kalamazoo College, Kalamazoo, Michigan

1983   Instructor in drawing, Castle Hill, Truro, Massachusetts

1984   Traveled in Sicily, Italy

1985   Died July 20, Provincetown, Massachusetts

ONE-PERSON EXHIBITIONS

Hugo Gallery, New York, New York 1947, 1950

Kootz Gallery, New York, New York 1952

Stable Gallery, New York, New York 1958

Martha Jackson Gallery, New York, New York 1959, 1972, 1973, 1976, 1977

Gallery Mayer, New York, New York 1960

Galerie Stadler, Paris, France 1960

Isaac Delgado Museum of Art, New Orleans, Louisiana 1960

Weatherspoon Gallery, University of North Carolina at Greensboro 1963

Tibor de Nagy, New York, New York 1963, 1964

The Arts Club of Chicago, Chicago, Illinois 1965

New Orleans Museum of Art, New Orleans, Louisiana 1974

Art Association of Newport, Newport, Rhode Island 1974

Oklahoma Art Center, Oklahoma City, Oklahoma 1974

Cherry Stone Gallery, Wellfleet, Massachusetts 1977, 1986

Long Point Gallery, Provincetown, Massachusetts 1977, 1979, 1983

Western Carolina University, Cullowhee, North Carolina 1978

University of North Carolina at Chapel Hill 1978

Andre Zarre, New York, New York 1978

Landmark Gallery, New York, New York 1979, 1982

Kalamazoo College, Kalamazoo, Michigan 1981

Barbara Fiedler Gallery, Washington, D.C. 1981

Gallery Schlesinger- Boisanté, New York, New York 1982, 1986, 1987

Portland Museum of Art, Portland, Maine 1987

Hunter College, New York, New York 1987

William Benton Museum of Art, University of Connecticut, Storrs, Connecticut 1989

Gallery Schlesinger, New York, New York 1989, 1990, 1991, 1992, 1993

Tilden-Foley Gallery, New Orleans, Louisiana 1989, 1991, 1993

Kouros Gallery, New York, New York 1991

SELECTED GROUP EXHIBITIONS

1949   *American Abstract Artists 13th Annual*, Riverside Museum, New York, New York
Forum '49, Gallery 200, Provincetown, Massachusetts

1950   *Virginia Museum Biennial*, Virginia Museum, Richmond Virginia
Annual Exhibition of Contemporary Art, Whitney Museum of American Art, New York, New York
B.O.W./ Black or White, Kootz Gallery, New York, New York
New Talent, Artist's Gallery, New York, New York
Realities Nouvelles, 5éme Salon, Palais des Beaux artes de la Ville de Paris, Paris, France
American Abstract Artists, Galleria Nationale d'Arte Moderna, Rome, Italy
Post Abstract Artists—France and America, Provincetown, Massachusetts

1951   *American Abstract Artists 15th Anniversary Exhibition*, New York, New York
Summer Souvenirs, Kootz Gallery, New York, New York

1952   *Annual Exhibition*, Whitney Museum of American Art, New York, New York
Fifth Annual Exhibition of Contemporary Painting, University of Illinois, Urbana, Illinois

1953   *Contemporary American Painting and Sculpture*, University of Illinois, Urbana, Illinois

1955   *Annual Exhibition*, Whitney Museum of American Art, New York, New York

1957   *Group Show*, Gutai 8, Osaka, Japan

1958   *An International Selection: Europe, Japan, United States*, Signa Gallery, East Hampton, New York
Some Younger Names in American Painting, Worcestor Art Museum, Worcester, Massachusetts
International Art of a New Era, Osaka Art Festival, Osaka, Japan
Collage in America, Zabriskie Gallery, New York, New York

1959   *Twenty Quadri*, Galleria della Ariete, Milan, Italy
Arte Nouva; International Exhibition of Painting and Sculpture, Turin, Italy
American Abstract Artists, Riverside Museum, New York, New York

1960   *The International Sky Festival*, Osaka, Japan
Sixty American Painters, Walker Art Center, Minneapolis, Minnesota
Neue Malerie, Städtische Galery, Munich, Germany
Group Show, Michel Warren Gallery, New York, New York

1961   *Five Painters from Paris*, Kölnisher Kunstverein, Cologne, Germany
Tenth Gutai Exhibition, Tokyo, Japan

1962   *Metamorphosis*, Galerie Stadler, Paris, France
Gutai Thirteen, Osaka, Japan
Strutture E Stile: Forty-two Artists of Europe, America and Japan, Turin, Italy

1963   *Fifth Annual Group Show*, Brookhaven National Labs, Brookhaven, New York
Provincetown, a Painter's Place, American Federation of Arts (traveling exhibition)

1964   *Sixty-seventh American Exhibition*, The Art Institute of Chicago, Chicago, Illinois

1965   *Selected Works from Tougaloo College*, Orleans Gallery, New Orleans, Louisiana
Fifty Artists—Fifty Oeuvres, Galerie Lutèce, Paris, France
XVII Salon de la Jeune Sculpture, Musée Nationale Rodin, Paris, France

1966   *Artists and Collectors Benefit for the City of Florence, Italy*, Capricorn Gallery, New York, New York
Variety: Group Show of Drawings, Fine Arts Gallery, Purdue University, West Lafayette, Indiana

1967   *Works of Art in the Collection of Nelson A. Rockefeller*, Rockefeller Gallery, Seal Harbor, Maine
Selection 1967; Recent Acquisitions, University of California, Berkeley, California

1968   *Painting as Painting*, The Art Museum, University of Texas at Austin, Austin, Texas
        The Collection, Tougaloo College, Tougaloo, Mississippi
        Ten Major American Painters, Tirca Karlis Gallery, Provincetown, Massachusetts

1969   *Artists Abroad*, Institute of International Education, New York, New York
        Five Artists—Collage, Purdue Art Department, Purdue University, West Lafayette, Indiana

1970   *American Painting, 1970*, Virginia Museum, Richmond, Virginia
        Five Faces of Fine Art, Alumni Exhibition, Newman School, New Orleans, Louisiana

1971   *Fifty-Six Artists*, Art New England, Boston Center for the Arts, Boston, Massachusetts

1973   *Drawing U.S.A.*, Minnesota Museum of Art, St. Paul, Minnesota
        Collection of Martha Jackson, University of Maryland, College Park, Maryland; Finch College
                Museum, New York, New York; Albright Knox Museum, Buffalo, New York
        Fourth National Drawing Invitational, University of Wisconsin, Green Bay, Wisconsin

1974   *Sculpture Competition*, Society of Fine Arts, Miami, Florida
        Contemporary Collage, Vassar College, Poughkeepsie, New York
        One Hundred and Eighteen Artists, Landmark Gallery, New York, New York

1975   *Twenty American Fulbright Artists*, Union Carbide Gallery, New York, New York

1976   *Forty Years of American Collage*, Buecker and Harpsichord Gallery, New York,
                New York; St. Peter's College, Jersey City, New Jersey
        Williams College Alumni Loan Exhibit, Hirschl and Adler Gallery, New York, New York;
                Williams College Museum of Art, Williamstown, Massachusetts
        Works on Paper from the Ciba-Geigy Collection, Wichita Falls Museum, Wichita Falls, Texas;
                Neuberger Museum, SUNY, Purchase, New York
        One Hundred and Eighteen Artists, Landmark Gallery, New York, New York

1977   *Provincetown Painters*, 1890's to 1970's, Everson Museum, Syracuse, New York
        Cape Cod as an Art Colony, Heritage Plantation, Sandwich, Massachusetts
        Three at Cherry Stone, Cherry Stone Gallery, Wellfleet, Massachusetts
        Perspective '77, Freedman Art Gallery, Albright College, Reading, Pennsylvania

1978   *Painting and Sculpture Today*, Indianapolis Museum of Art, Indianapolis, Indiana
        Days Lumberyard Studio Exhibition, Provincetown Art Association, Provincetown, Massachusetts
        Drawing the Line, Montclair Art Museum, Montclair, New Jersey
        90 x 30; A Festival of Small Sculpture, Martha Jackson Gallery, New York, New York

1979   *Hans Hofmann and his School*, Metropolitan Museum of Art, New York, New York
        Collage; American Masters, Montclair Art Museum, Montclair, New Jersey
        Fourteen Provincetown Artists of Today, University of Michigan, Ann Arbor, Michigan

1980   *One Hundred and Eighteen Artists*, Landmark Gallery, New York, New York

1981   *Tracking the Marvelous*, Grey Art Gallery and Study Center, New York, New York
        Classic Americans; XXth Century Painters and Sculptors, Stamford Museum, Stamford, Connecticut
        Recent Acquisitions, Montclair Art Museum, Montclair, New Jersey

1982   *The Judith Rothschild Collection*, Jewett Art Center, Wellesley, Massachusetts
        Contemporary Art at One Penn Plaza, One Penn Plaza, New York, New York
        Vanguard American Paintings of the 30's and 40's, Gallery Schlesinger-Boisanté,
                New York, New York

1983   *Hans Hofmann as Teacher*, American Federation of Arts, (traveled in United States)

1984   *Artists at Hunter*, Hunter college, New York, New York
        The New York Art Experience, 909 Third Avenue Lobby, New York, New York
        American Innovation, Part II, Gallery Schlesinger-Boisanté, New York, New York

1985   *Recent Trends in Collecting*, National Museum of American Art, Washington, D.C.
Peintres Américains, Galerie Stadler, Paris, France
New Acquisitions, Portland Museum of Art, Portland, Maine
A Tribute to Martha Jackson, Arbitrage Gallery, New York, New York
Two-man Show, Cherry Stone Gallery, Wellfleet, Massachusetts (with Robert Motherwell)
Profile of a Connoisseur, New Orleans Museum of Art, New Orleans, Louisiana

1985-6   *Figural Art of the New York School*, SUNY, Purchase, New York; Louisiana State University,
Baton Rouge, Louisiana

1986   *After Matisse*, The Queens Museum of Art, Flushing, New York; The Chrysler Museum,
Norfolk, Virginia; Portland Museum of Art, Portland, Maine
Crosscurrents, Provincetown Art Association, Provincetown, Massachusetts; Guild Hall,
Easthampton, New York
Hans Hofmann and his Legacy, Lever/Myerson Gallery, New York, New York
Drawings—Fritz Bultman and Joseph Albers, Cherry Stone Gallery, Wellfleet, Massachusetts

1987   *After Matisse*, Bass Museum of Art, Miami Beach, Florida; The Phillips Collection,
Washington, D.C.; Dayton Art Institute, Dayton, Ohio; Worcester Art
Museum, Worcester, Massachusetts
Works of the 30's and 40's, Gallery Schlesinger-Boisanté, New York, New York
Anne Ryan and Circle, Washburn Gallery, New York, New York

1988   *The Irascibles*, CDS Gallery, New York, New York
In Memory of John; Homage to John Myers, Kouros Gallery, New York, New York
Contemporary American Collage, 1960-1986, Herter Art Gallery, University of Massachusetts
at Amherst, Amherst, Massachusetts; William Benton Museum of Art, University of
Connecticut, Storrs, Connecticut; Lehigh Art Galleries, Bethlehem, Pennsylvania; The
Butler Institute of American Art, Youngstown, Ohio; SUNY, Albany, New York;
Nevada Institute of Contemporary Art, Las Vegas, Nevada
Art in the Garden, Cape Museum of Fine Arts, Dennis, Massachusetts
Abstraction, Gallery Schlesinger-Boisanté, New York, New York

1989   *Contemporary Provincetown*, Provincetown Art Association, Provincetown, Massachusetts;
Murray Feldman Gallery, West Hollywood, California
Group at Art 54, 54 Greene St. Gallery, New York, New York
Homage to Walter Chrysler; The Provincetown Years, Katzen-Brown Gallery,
New York, New York
Myth and Ritual, Long Point Gallery, Provincetown, Massachusetts

1990   *A Salute to the Signa Gallery*, Guild Hall, Easthampton, New York
The Provocative Years, 1935-1945; The Hans Hofmann School in Provincetown,
Provincetown Art Association, Provincetown, Massachusetts
From the Studio Wall, Long Point Gallery, Provincetown, Massachusetts
Major Works, Provincetown Art Association, Provincetown, Massachusetts

1991   *Art in the Garden*, Cape Museum of Fine Art, Dennis, Massachusetts
The Second Wave; American Abstraction of the 30's and 40's, The Yasuna Collection,
Worcester Art Museum, Worcester, Massachusetts
The Artist's Eye, Provincetown Art Association, Provincetown, Massachusetts

1992   *Papers*, Gallery Schlesinger, New York, New York
American Vanguard; Jackson Pollock, Lee Krasner and Friends, Stuart Levy Gallery,
New York, New York
Bultman, Motherwell and Tworkov, Cherry Stone Gallery, Wellfleet, Massachusetts

1993   *Selections from Williams College Alumni*, Williams College Museum of Art,
Williamstown, Massachusetts
Copenhagan—U.S.A., Copenhagen, Denmark
Celebrating Long Point, Station Gallery, Katohah, New York
Salute to Long Point, Stuart Levy Gallery, New York, New York

SELECTED BIBLIOGRAPHY

Weller, Allen S., *Contemporary American Painting and Sculpture*, (University of Illinois, 1953) pp. 171-72, plate 38

Arte Nouva, (Torino, Italy: 1959) p. 28

Alden, Daisy, *American Poems and Drawings* (New York; Folder Editions, 1959) p. 16

It Is, No. 3 (New York: Second Half Publishing Co., 1959) pp. 17, 53, 67

Tapié, Michel, *Morphologie Autre*, (Torino, Italy: Fratelli Possi, 1960)

"Bultman," *Aujourd'hui, Art et Architecture*, no. 27 (June, 1960), p. 48

Suro, Dario, *La Pintura en Neuva York*, (Madrid, Spain: Acento Cultural, 1960) pp. 46-48

Tapié, Michel, *Neue Malerei, form Struktur Bedeutung* (Munich, Germany: 1960) pp. 17-20

Gutai II, International Sky Festival (Osaka, Japan: Shozo Shimamoto, 1960) p. 15

Amason, H.H., *Sixty American Painters* (Minneapolis: Walker Art Center, 1960) pp. 53, 58

L'Illustration du XX Siècle (New York: Tudor Publishing Co., 1960) p. 91

Diehl, Gaston, *The Moderns* (New York: Crown Publishers, 1961) pp. 180, 210

Upton and Sedwick, *Highlights; An Illustrated History of Art*, (New York: Holt, Rinehart and Winston, 1963) p. 297

Bultman, Fritz, "The Achievement of Hans Hofmann," *Art News*, (New York: September, 1963) pp. 43-45, 54-55

American Exhibition (Chicago; The Art Institute of Chicago, 1964) p. 9

Seitz, William, *Contemporary Sculpture* (New York; Art Digest Inc., 1965) pp. 20-21

XVII Salon de la Jeune Sculpture (Paris, France: 1965) reproduced

Schlenoff, Norman, *Art in the Modern World* (Bantam Books: 1965) p. 215

Sedgwick, John P., Jr., *Discovering Modern Art* (New York; Random House, 1966) pp. 159-66

Selz, Peter, *Selection 1967* (Berkeley: University of California, 1967) p. 113

It Is, No. 6 (New York: Second Half Publishing Co., Autumn, 1968) p. 97

Artists Abroad (New York: American Federation of Arts, 1969), p. 98

Friedman, B.H. *Jackson Pollock; Energy Made Visible* (New York: McGraw Hill, 1972) pp. 71-72, 88, 152

Bultman, Fritz, "About my Drawings," *Texas Quarterly* (Austin. University of Texas, Spring 1973) p. 71-77

Stephens, Michael G., *Paragraphs* (Amherst: Mulch Press, 1974) fifteen drawings by Fritz Bultman reproduced

Turner, Stansfield, *Architectural Digest* (May-June, 1976) p. 20

The Fritz Bultman Calender, 1977 (Northampton: Mulch Press)

Friedman, B.H., "The Irascibles," *Arts Magazine* (September, 1978) pp. 96-102

"Fritz Bultman—Portfolio," *Cornell Review*, no. 6 (Ithaca: Cornell University, Summer 1979)
pp. 43-45, and cover page

Kingsley, April, "Opening and Closing: Fritz Bultman's Sculpture," *Arts Magazine* (New York: January,
1976) pp. 7-8

Masterpieces of Modern Art, [collection of Nelson Rockefeller], (Hudson Hill Press, 1981) p. 18

Firestone, Evan, "The Collages of Fritz Bultman," *Arts Magazine* (New York: December, 1981)
pp. 63-64

Myers, John Bernard, *Tracking the Marvelous* (New York: Grey Art Gallery and Study Center, April,
1981) p. 62

Simmons, Linda C. *American Drawings, Watercolors, Pastels and Collage* (Washington D.C.: Corcoran
Gallery of Art, 1983) plate 1464

Bultman, Fritz, "Possibilities for a Renewed Tradition of Catholic Art in the United States,"
New Catholic World (Paulist Press, 1984) pp. 29, 30, 31

Potter, Jeffrey, *To a Violent Grave* (New York; G.P. Putnam's Sons, 1985) pp. 63, 64-65, 67, 68, 77,
115, 123, 126, 141, 148, 153, 173, 203-04, 213, 279

Digby, Joan and John, *The Collage Handbook* (Thames and Hudson, 1985) pp. 105-07, color plate IV

Profile of a Connoisseur, (New Orleans: New Orleans Museum of Art, 1985) pp. 21-22, 50-52

Rand, Harry, *Martha Jackson Memorial Collection* (Washington D.C.; Smithsonian Institution Press,
1985) pp. 21-25

Ashton, Doré; Bell, Tiffany; Sandler, Irving, *After Matisse* (Independent Curators Inc., 1986) pp. 10, 54

Hopkins, Budd, "The Collages of Fritz Bultman," *Provincetown Arts* (Provincetown, Massachusetts:
July, 1986) pp. 11, 16

Friedman, B.H., "In Memorium," *Arts Magazine* (New York: January, 1986) pp. 78-79

Goodman, Cynthia, *Hans Hofmann* (New York: Abbeville Press, 1985) pp. 18, 31, 44, 48, 61, 63, 96

Naifeh, Stephen and Smith, Gregory White, *Jackson Pollock—An American Saga* (Clarkson and Potter
Inc., 1989) pp. 326, 371, 380-381, 419, 449, 477; Section J.P.: pp. 326, 406, 529, 551, 664-65;
Section L.K.: pp. 371, 381, 382, 388, 401, 402, 568, 708

LeClair, Charles, *Color in Contemporary Painting* (New York: Watson-Guptil Publications, 1991) pp.
125, 126, 127

Perl, Jed, "Breakthrough, Idyll, Icon, Allegory," *The New Criterion* (New York: May, 1992) p. 52

Kingsley, April, *The Turning Point* (New York: Simon and Schuster, 1992) pp. 83-86